THE TOP 11 OF EVERYTHING TOON

Newcastle United

IT'S NOT TRIVIA, IT'S MORE IMPORTANT THAN THAT

Written by
Paul Simpson, Alan Oliver, Mikey Carr

Text editors
Paul Simpson, Helen Rodiss,
Michaela Bushell

Production
Ian Cranna, Tim Oldham,
Andy Pringle

Cover and book design
Sharon O'Connor

Cover image
Charlie Best

Thanks to
John Rice, www.nufc.com,
Toonarama

Printed in Spain
by Graphy Cems

This edition published
July 2005 was prepared by
Haymarket Network for
Rough Guides Ltd,
80 Strand, London, WC2R ORL

**Distributed by the
Penguin Group**
Penguin Books Ltd,
27 Wrights Lane,
London W8 5TZ

A catalogue record for this
book is available from the
British Library

ISBN 1-84353-560-2

Contents

ROUGH GUIDE

11s

Newcastle United

Asked if Newcastle United was a cartoon character which one would it be?, fan Angus Batey told *The Times*:"Homer Simpson: much loved but destined to fail."

ABSOLUTE BEST MOMENTS

Days – and nights – when life seemed too good to be true

1. The night Newcastle United beat Barcelona

They say it was the greatest night in Newcastle United's history. 17 September 1997: the night mighty Barcelona came to St James' Park for United's first ever game in the Champions League proper. And were beaten 3-2 after an amazing hat-trick by Tino Asprilla. Kenny Dalglish had – with Kevin Keegan's team – taken Newcastle into the Champions League for the first time. A full house at St James' Park and 250 million TV viewers watched in disbelief as Newcastle strolled into a 3-0 lead, despite the absence of the injured Alan Shearer. Asprilla's first goal was a penalty. For his last two he rose like a salmon to head in right wing crosses from Keith Gillespie. Even late goals from Enrique and Figo could not spoil Newcastle's night.

2. Newcastle United win the Inter-Cities Fairs Cup

Newcastle United scraped into Europe for the first time in 1968/69 because of the rule that only one club per city could enter the Inter-Cities Fairs Cup. The Geordies didn't care as their side swept aside Feyenoord, Sporting Lisbon, Real Zaragoza, Vitoria Setubal and Rangers to set up a two-legged final with crack Hungarian outfit Ujpesti Dozsa. St James' Park was full to its 60,000 capacity as skipper Bobby Moncur, who had never scored a first-team goal before, hit the target twice as Joe Harvey's merry men, with another goal from Jimmy Scott, romped to a 3-0 win. After a week's wait, Newcastle were 2-0 down at half-time in the second leg in Budapest on 11 June 1969. But Moncur scored again – as did Benny Arentoft and Alan Foggon as Newcastle won the trophy 6-2 on aggregate. Tyneside went mad.

3. A crazy night in Rotterdam

When Newcastle United headed to Holland on 13 November 2002 they were on the brink of one of the greatest comebacks in Champions League history. They had lost their first three games in the first group stage, but had beaten Juventus and Dinamo Kyiv at St James Park. They knew even victory over Feyenoord would not be enough to take them through unless the Dynamo Kiev-Juventus result went their way. All Newcastle could do was win and it looked as though they were going to do so comfortably when Craig Bellamy and Hugo Viana put them 2-0 ahead. But Feyenoord scored twice. At this stage Newcastle, Feyenoord or Kiev could all have gone through but Bellamy scored a late winner. Sir Bobby Robson's Newcastle had created a very Toon kind of Champions League history by becoming the first side to qualify for the second group stage after losing their first three matches.

4. The 1955 FA Cup win
Newcastle had won the FA Cup in 1951 and 1952. Surely it was asking too much for them to make it a 1950s hat-trick in 1955? Especially as manager Duggie Livingstone dropped the 1951 two-goal hero Jackie Milburn before the Wembley final with Manchester City. Newcastle have always made the news and did so again when Stan Seymour and his board reinstated Wor Jackie. Milburn, not the greatest header of a ball, nodded in a corner from the right after 45 seconds and City were beaten 3-1. Fifty years on, Newcastle are still waiting for their next domestic trophy.

5. The humiliation of Manchester United
When Manchester United arrived at St James' Park on 20 October 1996, Newcastle fans needed no reminder that Alex Ferguson's side had eaten away a 12 point gap to pip them for the title the season before. Newcastle wanted revenge but no-one anticipated this 5-0 drubbing of the Red Devils, with goals from Darren Peacock, David Ginola, Les Ferdinand, Alan Shearer and Philippe Albert. Who will ever forget Albert's cheeky chip over the top of Peter Schmeichel to complete the rout?

6. The signing of Alan Shearer
When Kevin Keegan resurrected Newcastle United, one thing was missing – a talismanic goalscorer. And if there was one player in the world Newcastle fans wanted in the summer of 1996 more than anyone it was Alan Shearer. Luckily, Shearer wanted to come home. A then world-record fee of £15m was cheap for a player who was to become arguably the greatest in the club's history.

7. The signing of Kevin Keegan
Newcastle United were going nowhere in the early 1980s so not many Geordies believed reports that they were going to sign the then England captain – and twice European Footballer of the Year – Kevin Keegan. But sure enough a packed press conference at Tyneside's leading hotel was told by secretary Russell Cushing: "We're in heaven, we've got Kevin." Keegan cost £100,000 from Southampton in August

1982 and almost single-handedly revitalised the fortunes of Newcastle United, culminating with promotion in 1983/84 before he retired to Spain.

8. The return of Kevin Keegan

In 1992 United were hurtling towards the old Third Division and so deep in debt there was talk of the club dying. Only one man could save them. Kevin Keegan. After a dismal 5-2 defeat at Oxford United early in February, Ossie Ardiles was sacked and, for the second time, Keegan answered an SOS from Newcastle United. Out of the game since 1984, he staved off relegation that season, won promotion the next and took Newcastle back into Europe for the first time in 17 years.

9. Malcolm Macdonald's home debut

Newcastle fans took to Malcolm Macdonald when he arrived on Tyneside in the summer of 1981 after his £180,000 transfer from Luton Town in a white Rolls Royce. And they took to him even more after his hat-trick on his home debut against Liverpool. Nobody could have written the script. Supermac had arrived.

10. Farewell to the First Division

Newcastle United were already promoted by the time Leicester City came to St James' Park to close the 1992/93 season. Not surprisingly there was a carnival atmosphere. And what a party it was as Newcastle hammered Leicester 7-1 after being 6-0 up at the interval as Kevin Keegan and Terry McDermott danced around on the touchline. Both David Kelly and Andy Cole scored hat-tricks.

11. Beardsley destroys Manchester City

Newcastle won promotion in 1984 mainly off the back of some of the most exciting forward play seen at St James' Park from Kevin Keegan, Peter Beardsley and Chris Waddle. Nothing epitomises that trio more than the 5-0 bashing of promotion rivals Manchester City in October 1983. On this occasion, Beardsley grabbed the glory with a hat-trick. This 5-0 victory had promotion written all over it.

ALL-TIME TOP GOALSCORERS

They've hit the net more often than a tennis player with a dodgy forehand

1. **Jackie Milburn** 200 goals in 399 appearances
2. **Alan Shearer** 192 goals in 355 appearances
3. **Len White** 153 goals in 270 appearances
4. **Hughie Gallacher** 143 goals in 174 appearances

5. Malcolm Macdonald 121 goals in 228 appearances
6. Peter Beardsley 118 goals in 320 appearances
7. Tom McDonald 113 goals in 367 appearances
8. Bobby Mitchell 113 goals in 410 appearances
9. Neil Harris 101 goals in 194 appearances
10. Bryan 'Pop' Robson 97 goals in 243 appearances
11. Jackie Rutherford 94 goals in 336 appearances

AROUND THE WORLD WITH UNITED

11 United stars you'll find on a map

Harry Bedford 1930-1932
Maurice Blackburn 1939-1941
Robert Blackburn 1906-1908
Thomas Blyth 1896-1898
Gary Brazil 1989-1990
Ollie Burton 1963-1973
Henry Clifton 1938-1946
Jimmy Denmark 1937-1946
Christopher Holland 1994-1996
Harry Ware 1935-1937
David Whitton 1892-1893

> THE MINK ROSETTES,
> FROM A FARM IN
> NORTHUMBERLAND,
> COST JUST 75P IN 1971
> FROM THE CLUB SHOP

ARTEFACTS

11 obscure objects of desire connected to the Magpies

1. A signed first edition of Jackie Milburn's autobiography, Golden Goals
This could cost around £80, but here's one artefact that we can see the point of.

2. A Royal Doulton Newcastle United Subbuteo player
Why pay £90 for a Subbuteo player you can never flick?

3. A signed photo of Vinnie grabbing Gazza's balls
A snip at £130 – although the picture of Gazza with the flyaway hair, tree-trunk thighs, and silver strip with star is probably funnier still.

4. A rare silver Newcastle shirt
An Umbro kit experiment in the 1980s, so rare some collectors sell them for £650.

5. The Alan Shearer 12in ruler
When Alan finally does hang up his boots, who else is going to shift rulers from the club shop? The Kieron Dyer 12in ruler just sounds rude.

6. A mink rosette
They cost 75p from the club shop, were fashionable in 1971/72 and came all the way from a mink farm in Northumberland.

7. The Newcastle United ladies pyjamas
In tasteful pale blue and white. But get in there because sizes 8-14 sell out quickly.

8. The Malcolm Macdonald mug
Think of Supermac everytime you have a coffee. Just £14.99 including postage.

9. A Newcastle shirt worn by Craig Bellamy
Available in an online emporium for £135. They might have to drop the price.

10. The empty 10in print
A stirring view of St James' Park in a wooden frame bulkier than Micky 'Sumo' Quinn.

11. Souvenir record of the 1976 League Cup final
In good nick, yours for just £12, but, as United lost 2-1, not worth the asking price.

BAD BOYS
Villains, rogues, pugilists in black and white

1. Craig Bellamy
Norman Stanley Fletcher probably has a shorter rap sheet than Craig Bellamy. Mouthing "Premiership" to Wolves after Newcastle had lost to them in the FA Cup,

speculating on whether he'd feign injury to avoid playing out of position, being cautioned for assault on a woman, sending gloating text messages to his old striking partner saying, in effect, "You're finished", not shaking hands with opponents, boasting about his wages on the pitch – it's an impressive record. One thing about Craig, he's not subtle. If he's going to make a prat of himself, he'll do it o camera if humanly possible. All that said, he can't half play.

2. Kieron Dyer
Punches like a girl, drives like a madman – no bridge is safe when our Kieron's behind the wheel. Known to urinate in the street, he once admitted he'd lost count of how many partners he'd had on a night of mattress-surfing in Cyprus, so maybe the video he took with Rio Ferdinand and Frank Lampard was an aide memoire. An link between this evidence of a hectic private life and his mysterious failure to fulfil his promise as England's most exciting midfielder is, of course, just coincidental.

3. Hughie Gallacher
Trained hard, played hard, known to have a pint at the Strawberry Inn just before a match, Wee Hughie was often spotted by United trainer Andy McCombie "canned up on a Friday" but still banged the ball in the net on a Saturday. On a disastrous tou of Europe in 1929, one referee moaned "I was standing quite close to the player [Gallacher] and I am quite convinced he was quite tipsy… I heard he drank much cognac between the two halves." He also, under the influence, traded blows under a bridge in the city and ended up in court. So when tough disciplinarian manager Andy Cunningham came in, Gallacher's time at St James' Park was up.

4. Keith Gillespie
In 1996, the Newcastle squad were told their flying winger was £60,000 in debt to the bookies. But Gillespie, said John Beresford, "was very matter of fact about it all. I it'd been me I would have been in pieces." He had, it was alleged, helped arrange bets for other staff at Manchester United and once admitted to gambling away £47,000 in a single day. At Leicester, eight years later, he was one of three players charged with sexual misdeeds in a Spanish hotel. The charges were later dropped.

5. Douglas Hall and Freddy Shepherd
Toongate! Doug, who deserves the credit for persuading dad to fire Ossie and hire Keegan, showed his remorse by quitting, keeping out of sight and shaving off his moustache. Freddy seems, in contrast, to have become addicted to publicity.

6. Jamie McClen
Young midfielder, fined by the club in February 2002 after a late-night fracas in the

city centre and released in 2005. News of his fracas – and Bellamy's caution – prompted Freddy Shepherd to say he had had enough of seeing players plastered over the front pages. That, clearly, is the chairman's prerogative.

7. Albert Shepherd

The only Magpie to have been dropped from an FA Cup semi-final because the board believed he'd been bribed to throw the game. The rumours persisted but, in the absence of proof, threat of a players' strike forced his reinstatement and, after a replay, Newcastle beat Barnsley in 1910 to lift the FA Cup. Often referred to as a character who liked to showboat and drink – make of that what you will.

8. Lee Bowyer

Failed to live down to media expectations at St James' Park until he started throwing punches. In that respect, he resembles Big Dunc whose Drunken Ferguson stereotype didn't quite tally with his behaviour at Newcastle. As for Bowyer and Dyer, Lee shouldn't have taken it personally – Dyer just doesn't have the tactical nous required to spot a team-mate in a good position to receive the ball.

9. Paul Gascoigne

A bad boy in Newcastle after he left the club – too many tales of him winding up locals by chatting up their girlfriends, crawling around pubs, doing his damaged knee in – he was not unreasonably out of order while at United. He was almost chinned for pranks on team-mates and his diet was so atrocious he looked, at one point, more like the next Billy Bunter than the new George Best. But, let's be honest, the worst thing he ever did at Newcastle was leave.

10. James Stevenson

A wizard of an inside-right in the Victorian era, his Newcastle career lasted just a season. Injury was the official excuse but trainer Tom Dodds's report to the board on the players in January 1899 told a different story. Dodds noted: "Stevenson: worse for liquor at Glossop match, absent from training".

11. John Burridge

Casting himself as a loveable eccentric, nomadic Budgie used to wear his goalkeeping gloves in bed. Such was his interest in leisure wear that he was convicted of selling counterfeit gear to players while player/manager of Blyth Spartans. He pleaded poverty. John Beresford recalls that going to an estate agent with Burridge would be dangerous: "He came with me to an estate agents in Durham and a couple of girls recognised me, so I said 'Hello.' John came over and immediately started to strip off. It was the middle of December and he stripped down to virtually nothing, showing off his muscles, saying to the girls how well he looked after himself and that they should be looking at him. I just cringed in the corner and wished I was somewhere else." Quite.

Manager: Kevin Keegan
Despite being "the Julie Andrews of football", as Duncan McKenzie dubbed him, King Kev was not averse to the odd tipple. After a long lunch with the press as manager, the strains of his karaoke version of *My Way* could be heard ringing through a local hotel. And his bid to wean his Entertainers off beer – and educate their palette with some decent white wine – backfired so badly that, after one away game, he ended up drinking the wine himself and had to be carried off the coach.

BANJOS, BARN DOORS AND SUCH (1)

11 seasons when Newcastle hit the target least often

1. 1980/81 30 goals
2. 1988/89 32 goals
3. 1997/98 35 goals
4. 1913/14 39 goals
4. 1966/67 39 goals
6. 1900/01 41 goals
7. 1900/01 42 goals
7. 1977/78 42 goals
9. 1919/20 44 goals
10. 1970/71 44 goals
11. 2000/01 44 goals
Stats only apply to league games, there's no sense in piling on the misery, is there?

BANJOS, BARN DOORS AND SUCH (2)

Iffy strikers listed by the utterly subjective criteria of how much they annoyed us

1. Billy Whitehurst 30 games, 7 goals
Billy hated Newcastle. "The fans were a bag of shit, the players weren't worth a light. I used to be at the dogs all the time." Sorry Billy, but with your strike rate in 1985/86, you'd gone to the dogs before we shelled out £232,500 on you.

11. BARCELONA !

Shay Given

John Beresford   Warren Barton
    Steve Watson   Philippe Albert

Keith Gillespie   David Batty   Rob Lee   John Barnes

    Tino Asprilla   Jon Dahl Tomasson

Freddie Mercury's anthem was obviously written for this line-up which humbled the mighty Barcelona on 13 September 1997 in the Champions League

2. Bobby Shinton 47 games, 10 goals
He mesmerised defenders for Wrexham and antagonised fans at St James' Park although, to be fair, he had the misfortune to have one of the least effective striking partners (Ray Clarke) in the club's history and to play upfront in 1980/81, one of the most boring seasons the club has ever known.

3. Ray Clarke 18 games, 3 goals
Ray was unlucky on two counts. He was replacing prolific Peter Withe and playing for United in 1980/81. He fed off the kind of delicate passes and touches he had been used to in Holland and Belgium but, aside from Chris Waddle, there was nothing delicate about the team he joined.

4. Ian Rush 9 games, 2 goals
Past it when he followed King Kenny to St James' Park to play nine games. In years to come, his Newcastle career will come to seem like a mirage – to him and us.

5. Stephane Guivarc'h 2 games, 1 goal
Signed by Dalglish, derided on TV by Gullit who then inherited him as a player, he scored on his debut against Liverpool in 1998/99 – shame that they scored four in

return – and only played one more game. He was later dropped in favour of Paul Dalglish and found loitering miserably in the car park during a League Cup match against Tranmere. He was quickly sold to Rangers and later retired through injury.

6. Carl Cort 24 games, 8 goals
Not a bad strike rate, but 24 games in four years?

7. Chris Guthrie 4 games, 0 goals
Unlucky to be vying with Supermac for a first-team place. After seven goals in six games as a schoolboy international, his Newcastle record of played 4 scored 0 was a bit of a comedown. But he had a decent spell at Southend later.

8. Paul Moran 1 game, 0 goals
Known as Sparrow at Spurs, this loan signing missed a sitter on his home debut in February 1991 and never played for the first team again.

9. Jon Dahl Tomasson 27 games, 4 goals
Hard to believe this is the same bloke who popped up in the Champions League semi-final to nick a second for Milan against PSV.

10. Joe Allon 10 games, 2 goals
Joe scored nearly 120 goals in less than 150 games for the reserves but was never really given a chance in the first team. Should have been more prolific – his hair and teeth were enough to scare most defences.

11. Billy Rafferty 37 games, 8 goals
A tall, leggy striker who could trouble defenders, Rafferty wasn't totally crap or bone idle but, in 1985/86, just not good enough, scoring six goals in 34 league games.

BARNET FC

A team of hair don'ts in alphabetical order

1. Joe Allon
Big blond hair and big teeth, could have been a racehorse.

2. Warren Barton
Little Lord Fauntleroy fop which led cynics to underestimate his defensive prowess.

3. Peter Beardsley
A bowl cut, somewhere between early Beatles and medieval monk's standard issue.

4. John Brownlie
Seminal bubble perm with the bubbles packed tighter than in a bar of Aero.

5. David Ginola
A magnifique hairstyle as sculpted as the Arc de Triomphe.

6. Gary Kelly
Big 1980s hair didn't quite disguise this keeper's lack of height on crosses.

7. Temuri Ketsbaia
The slaphead look perfectly accentuated his look of serial-killer intensity.

8. Brian Kilcline
The definitive long hair and walrus moustache combo.

9. Malcolm Macdonald
With Supermac's supersideburns, he could have joined a Mungo Jerry tribute band.

10. Bobby Mitchell
Flying down the wing, Bobby acquired what one fan called a full Cornetto hairstyle.

11. Chris Waddle
The full mullet wasn't in flower at St James' Park but the warning signs were there.

BEER, BEEF FLUID AND BURGERS
11 sordid commercial endorsements

1. Barclays Bank
Sir Bobby Robson riding a bus and endorsing Barclays Bank.

2. Black and white shoes
Made by Northampton shoemakers Frank Wright for the 1974 FA Cup finalists.

3. Frank Brennan's sports shop
In the good old days, players often opened sports shops either just before retiring or

after. Frank, the best central defender United may have ever had, opened his, in Gallowgate, while still on the club's books, with dire consequences (see: Bust Ups).

4. L'Oreal
Daveed needs L'Oreal because, as he famously admitted, his hair is really grey.

5. McDonalds
Alan Shearer showed his usual commitment to master – alright, grasp the basics – of the actor's art to star in these long running, reasonably funny ads for McDonalds. If Supermac had played 20 years later, he could have had a burger named after him.

6. Malcolm Macdonald
Supermac's imaginatively entitled boutique in Newgate shopping precinct "catered for the exclusive man", offering such sartorial treats as a white suit made by John Peter of London.

7. Oxo
James McPherson, trainer of the great Newcastle side of Edwardian times, reckoned that: "Oxo gives great staying power to the players, so much so, that it is my intention to again use no other form of beef fluid during this season."

8. Pizza Hut
Chris Waddle, Gareth Southgate and Stuart Pearce joke over missed penalties and sell pizza. Waddle denies it took Gareth 27 takes to get his lines right. "It was a long day but I don't remember how many takes. Stuart and I were too busy eating pizza to notice." Funny the first few times – like Gazza spurting tears for Walkers Crisps.

9. Quaker Oats
Endorsed by Jackie Milburn, feeling hard up despite being one of the most famous footballers of the 1950s.

10. Milburn's Tours
Wor Jackie's coach-touring business – he also ran a fireplace shop for a while.

11. Tartan bitter
This brown, turgid bitter was, so the ads proudly declared, "The Macdonald Tartan". Supermac promoted it heavily, much to the annoyance of his manager Gordon Lee.

BEST FINISHES

The Toon's finest seasons in the old Division One/brand spanking new Premiership

1. 1926/27 1st 56 points
2. 1908/09 1st 53 points
3. 1906/07 1st 51 points
4. 1904/05 1st 48 points
5. 1995/96 2nd 78 points
6. 1996/97 2nd 68 points
7. 1993/94 3rd 77 points
8. 2002/03 3rd 69 points
9. 1911/12 3rd 44 points
10. 1901/02 3rd 37 points
11. 2001/02 4th 71 points

BOARD SILLY

11 own goals by the directors – yep. just 11

1. The injunction against the News Of The World

Let's be extremely charitable and say that everyone's had a few too many and said things they shouldn't, but who advised Freddy Shepherd and Douglas Hall to sue the *News Of The World* to stop the paper publishing their ruminations about the ugliness of local girls, gullibility of stupid fans, and boring strikers? As the judge said, dismissing the case,"If someone wants to keep something confidential, talking about it in a Spanish brothel is not the way to do it".

2. Handbags for the FA Cup

So elated were directors when United won the 1951 FA Cup, they bought a job lot of handbags for £17 and gave them to players' wives on the bandstand at the city's Oxford Galleries. The handbags were stuffed full with old newspaper clippings.

3. Banning transfer requests

Morale was so high in 1961 – seven players had asked to leave between August and October – that the board decided to ban players from making such requests.

4. "Regret none available, Newcastle United"

The Newcastle board's telegrammed reply to a request by Jimmy Nelson, who had captained the 1932 FA Cup final winning team, for tickets to the 1952 FA Cup final.

5. The Bowyer and Bellamy affairs
Tawdriness so badly mishandled by the board we're too tired to wisecrack.

6. Frankly appalling
In 1956, former player and manager/director Stan Seymour decided to reward Frank Brennan for his long service – 349 appearances in all competitions, once playing on while concussed – by cutting his weekly wage from £15 to £8.

7. Evicting the fans
In 2000, United needed more corporate hospitality – so the club decided to evict fans who held bonds entitling them to sit in the space where the club wanted to house the prawn-sandwich brigade. This battle eventually went to the High Court.

8. Blowing an FA Cup semi-final
In 1947, facing Charlton in the FA Cup semi-final, the directors decided to drop out-of-form Charlie Wayman, who had averaged 30 goals a season, for new boy George Stobbart. The players walked onto the pitch in a state of near mutiny and lost 4-0. A year later, Newcastle had one of the most talented, free-scoring forward lines in the club's history. So the directors destroyed it. Len Shackleton was summoned from the golf course to be told he was now playing for Sunderland. And winger Tommy Pearson was sold through guilt by association – he'd talked to Shack too much.

9. Fire the gaffer, but only after he's exhausted the transfer kitty
In the summer of 1998, Kenny Dalglish spent £16m on eight players and, by 27 August, had left the club in a resignation/firing so complex the courts had to sort it out. In the year and one day Ruud was in charge, he ran up another £10m deficit in transfers, before resigning. Last summer Sir Bobby was given £8m to spend – even though the board were already unconvinced he was the man for the job.

10. The great boardroom feud
Newcastle directors have often whinged about the lack of team spirit among their players. If any Newcastle player needed an object lesson in the art of not pulling together, they need only to read up on the history of the club in the 70 years since Frank Watt died. Boardroom feuding reached a senseless climax in the late 1950s when Willie McKeag and Stan Seymour both 'spoke' for the club. The absurd double act's finest hour was Charlie Mitten's reign as manager. He was hired by McKeag in June 1958 and fired by Seymour while McKeag was on holiday in October 1961.

11. Hiring Ossie Ardiles, Richard Dinnis, Jack Charlton...
The board could plead ignorance with Ossie but their knees must have gone all

11. BEST PREMIERSHIP GAME EVER

Pavel Srnicek

John Beresford   Philippe Albert

Steve Howey   Steve Watson
(Darren Peacock),

David Batty   Rob Lee   David Ginola

Peter Beardsley

Faustino Asprilla

Les Ferdinand

Best Premiership game ever
The side that played in the
seven-goal thriller at Anfield
in April 1996 – voted the
best Premiership game ever
by fans in 2003

trembly as Newcastle hurtled towards Division Three. Richard Dinnis – appointed in 1977 after the players gave the board an ultimatum – was well out of his depth – and Jack Charlton's teams never played a style of football the fans would warm to.

BOBBY DAZZLER
Words of wisdom – and other kinds of words – from Sir Bobby

1. "I can't sit there laughing, can I? Is that what you want? Ha ha ha – like that? Oh, penalty, ha, ha. Oh, it's saved. Ha ha. No it's gone in. Ha ha. What do you expect me to look like?"
Sir Bobby's hilarious response when asked about his downcast expression in 2003. Even when managing England in the 1980s, he was described as "having the natural expression of a man who suspects he's left the gas on at home".

2. "I would have given my right arm to have been a pianist"

3. "We're in a dogfight and the fight in the dog will get us out of trouble"

4. "They can't be monks – we don't want them to be monks; we want them to be football players because a monk doesn't play football at this level"

5. "Everyone's got tough games coming up – Manchester United have got Arsenal, Arsenal have got Manchester United and Leeds have got Leeds"

6. "Some of the goals were good, some of the goals were sceptical"

7. "We mustn't be despondent. We don't have to play them every week – although we do play them next week as it happens"

8. "Kevin Dyer"
Sir Bobby's name for Kieron Dyer, closer than his name for Shola Ameobi: "Carl Cort".

9. "He's got his legs back, of course – or his leg – he's always had one but now he's got two"

10. "We can't replace Gary Speed – where do you get an experienced player like him with a left foot and a head?"

11. "Anything from 1-0 to 2-0 would be a nice result"

BODY OF MEN

A Newcastle line-up you can find on your personage

1. Arthur Bottom
Inside-right who saved Newcastle from the drop in 1958 and had his own song with the crucial line "He shoots so hard, no one can stop them/Arthur Arthur Bottom".

> ARTHUR'S SONG:
> "HE SHOOTS SO HARD
> NO ONE CAN STOP
> THEM. ARTHUR,
> ARTHUR BOTTOM"

2. George Mole
Scored once in 1900 on his only game for United.

3. George Hair
Winger signed for ten guineas in 1943.

4. John Hynd
Goalkeeper in 1894/1895.

5. Wilf Innerd
A centre-half who played three games for Newcastle in 1901-1905.

6. Ian Bogie
Played in the same youth team as Gazza and, with his surname, must have suffered.

7. Wilfred Bott
A nippy winger who scored a fantastic hat-trick on his debut against Bury in 1935.

8. Robert Whitehead
With Newcastle from 1954 to 1962, this right-back's career at St James' Park was less conspicuous than the small white spots which plague teenage acne sufferers.

9. Alan Shoulder
Dragged from the pit – via Blyth Spartans – to partner Peter Withe upfront in 1978.

10. Bill Hart
A right half, described as "the ultimate terrier" by a team-mate.

11. Raymond Scarr
An inside-forward who played for Newcastle in World War 2.

BRING 'EM BACK

11 things fans miss about matchdays

1. Turning up for home games five minutes before kick-off knowing you'd get in.
2. Kenny Wharton sitting on the ball (see: Unusual Distinctions).
3. The bloke in the East stand who hollered like a Red Indian.
4. The open tunnel where you could ruffle Kev's hair as he ran onto the pitch.
5. The little men on the scoreboard that danced when Newcastle scored.
6. Being able to move to another bit of the ground if there was a nutter behind you.
7. Singing "We've got more fans than you" at away games.
8. Jackie Milburn.
9. The passion at midweek night games – especially in the Fairs Cup.
10. Match programmes costing six old pence.
11. "Peanuts a tanner a bag".

This selection is adapted from a fine survey conducted by fansite **www.nufc.com**.

BUST UPS, ARGIE BARGIES AND RELIGIOUS WARFARE

To avoid repetition, we have not detailed Bowyer v Dyer (see Bad Boys for more)

1. Craig Bellamy v Alan Shearer
"The chairman wishes to make it clear that Alan Shearer has never said to him he would knock seven bells out of anyone". Craig will be relieved to know that the worst he can expect is to have six bells knocked out of him.

2. Graeme Souness v Craig Bellamy, Aaron Hughes, Laurent Robert
The hard man claims to have only fallen out with five players as a manager. So how come he's had run-ins with three at St James' Park? Bellamy could start a row in an empty dressing room, and Robert has his moments, but shipping Aaron Hughes out to Aston Villa after eight years service without even a phone call? Why?

3. Kevin Keegan v John Beresford
Bez didn't like doing the defensive chores David Ginola wouldn't do. Keegan didn't like Bez whingeing about it. These views clashed spectacularly at Villa Park in April 1996, with Beresford shouting at his boss: "I told you he wouldn't f***king track back". The two made up, though Beresford was stunned to be left off the bench for the next game. When challenged, Keegan admitted that he was so used to having Bez in his first team, he'd forgotten he could have put him on the bench.

4. Malcolm Macdonald v Gordon Lee
"I loved Newcastle until Gordon Lee arrived," moaned Supermac. The manager with the skull-shaped head wanted no stars at St James' Park, so Supermac and Terry Hibbit had to go. Lee took the odd step of inciting other players to pick on the club's star striker. His number two Richard Dinnis tore a strip off Supermac in front of the other players after a 5-0 defeat by Wolves in April 1976, to which Supermac responded: "You have done nothing to help this club and nor has he," pointing at Lee's fleeing figure. Star and manager would be gone within the year.

5. Kevin Keegan v Alan Hudson
Losing 1-0 to Chelsea at Stamford Bridge in December 1995 was bad enough, then Alan Hudson had to slam Keegan's players. Keegan was so incensed that, says John Beresford, "Terry Mac had to physically restrain him as KK was up for decking the bloke. We were right behind him saying 'Go on gaffer' but it never came to blows."

6. Ruud Gullit v Rob Lee
"Ruud loved conflict: he loved being at loggerheads with players." So said the club's No37, Rob Lee, who was stripped of his captaincy by the Dutchman. But Lee had the

last laugh when the fans rallied to his defence and, in his autobiography, revealed that the flamboyant genius felt male pubic hair was unhygienic.

7. Kevin Keegan v Micky Quinn

Sumo had pictures of Keegan on his wall as a kid, so it was even more gutting when he realised that, as Newcastle manager, his idol didn't think he'd cut it in the big league. Quinn opened up to the tabloids, was confined to what he called "football purgatory" and sold to Coventry City. In public, Sumo says: "These things happen in football," in private, he sticks pins in his Kevin Keegan voodoo doll every night.

8. Stan Seymour v Frank Brennan, Willie McKeag

A genius on the wing, and a rogue elephant in the boardroom, Stan Seymour had some great moments as a Newcastle director – like telling his manager to stick Wor Jackie back in the team for the 1955 FA Cup final – but lost the plot too. His treatment of Frank Brennan, whose major crime was to open a sports shop which might compete with Seymour's, was shabby. His boardroom war with Willie McKeag over the Mr Newcastle naming rights was just plain unedifying.

9. Kevin Keegan v Andy Cole, Lee Clark

Two players who got on the wrong side of Keegan and never found their way back onto his right side. Clark's crime – kicking the bucket as he stormed down the touchline after being substituted against Southampton in October 1993 – was a crime of passion. In the same month, Andy Cole wanted to see his pals in London, Keegan refused to let him go and, after the striker had looked as useless in training as he has since done upfront for Fulham, told Cole: "If you don't want to play for us, you can clear off." Cole called Keegan's bluff, went AWOL, was recalled and helped United beat Wimbledon in the league. But within 15 months, Cole was sold.

10. Alan Shearer v Keith Gillespie

"Horseplay" was how Keith Gillespie's agent described an incident in February 1998 which left the winger in hospital with concussion after banging his head against a kerb outside a Dublin nightspot. Other accounts have Gillespie irritating Shearer to the point that, after a final warning, Alan felt obliged to deck the pesky Ulsterman.

11. Dominic Kelly v Jock Park

In 1938, Kelly, a staunch Irish Catholic, squared up to Park, a Protestant from Lanarkshire, and grabbed him by the throat shouting "Say 'God bless the Pope!'" Park roared back: "God bless King Billy!" The two had to be separated and directors banned discussion of religion for the rest of the season.

CAPTAIN MARVELS

Not all of whom have got their hands on the trophies they deserved

1. **Joe Harvey** FA Cup 1951, 1952
2. **Bobby Moncur** Inter-Cities Fairs Cup, 1969
3. **Colin Veitch** FA Cup 1910
4. **Andy Aitken** League champions 1905
5. **Frank Hudspeth** FA Cup 1924
6. **Bill McCracken** League champions 1907, 1909
7. **Kevin Keegan**
8. **Jimmy Scoular** FA Cup 1955
9. **Rob Lee**
10. **Alan Shearer**
11. **Jimmy Nelson** FA Cup 1932

CLEOPATRA'S NOSE MOMENTS

Marc Anthony was so smitten by Cleopatra's nose it changed history. Here are eleven moments that changed United

1. The dressing-room peg
Striker Charlie Wayman flounces out of St James' Park because he can't find a peg in the dressing room to hang his gear on. Getting the bus in from a pit village, he arrives to find all pegs are taken. The peg – added to his resentment at being dropped for an FA Cup semi-final – leads him to quit. In the emergency, the club shift a promising youngster called Jackie Milburn from the wing to No9.

2. Joe Harvey's tactical innovation
Two days before the 1974 FA Cup final, Newcastle switch from 4-3-3 to 4-4-2. With four in midfield, Macdonald and Tudor can't push the ball to the wings and wait for

the return. With no wingers, they can't exploit the Liverpool full-backs' vulnerability to pace. Newcastle are destroyed, Harvey quits, Gordon Lee arrives and a side which Jackie Milburn said was "just two players away from great" never fulfils its potential.

3. The Mexican wave

Wonderland songs, boos, Blaydon Races are all authentic St James' Park pastimes. But against Athletic Bilbao, in the 1994/95 UEFA Cup, the home fans start a Mexican wave with Newcastle 3-0 up with 30 minutes left. The result? The Basques snatch two late goals, win their home game 1-0 and win on away goals. United win only two of the next 12 league games; a season's promise evaporates.

4. Kevin Phillips's goal for Sunderland against Newcastle

Alan Shearer on the bench, Robert Lee so unwelcome he's watching some of the game at home praying Newcastle will lose, Ruud Gullit saying the Tyne and Wear derby isn't as good as Milan's local tussle… a bad scene. Newcastle lose 2-1, Kevin Phillips grabbing a 74th-minute winner. The defeat and the benching of the Geordie nation's representative on Earth force the board to see that Ruud's sexy football is a mirage. Bobby Robson takes charge, becoming the first manager to challenge in the Premiership since Keegan. All thanks to a Mackem striker.

5. Ernie Taylor requests a transfer

Fed up at not being picked against Celtic in a friendly in November 1951, Ernie Taylor asks for a transfer. The board, with that brand of hypocritical pomposity you only find in old-style football club directors and members of the FA council, decides it can't be dictated to by a player and lets Taylor go. Joe Harvey's plea ("Stan, for God's sake, don't give the fella a transfer, transfer me, transfer anybody, but keep Ernie") is ignored. Taylor, a scheming inside-forward, had helped inspire Newcastle's 1951 FA Cup run and would win the FA Cup in 1953 with Blackpool. In selling Taylor, the board begins to unpick a team that could have dominated English football.

6. John Hall takes a bath

And decides, according to Colin Malam's book *Magnificent Obsession: Keegan, Sir John Hall, Newcastle And Sixty Million Pounds*, that the club has to buy Andy Cole. He gets out of the bath and tells his wife: "Mae, we're going to have to buy Andy Cole and you're going to have to fund this one." Cole's goals power Newcastle into the new Premiership. The rest, as they say, is history, sometimes tragic, sometimes farcical, but better history than the club experienced in the old Division Two.

7. David Ginola's elbow

Against Arsenal, in a League Cup quarter-final in January 1996, Ginola plays with no protection from the referee who books him for diving. Frustrated, the Frenchman elbows Lee Dixon in the face. For John Beresford, as he told *nufc.com*, "That was in many ways the beginning of the end for him – he stopped being a team player, things got too personal with him, and he frustrated his team-mates as much as the other team." And when Ginola begins to sputter, so does the team.

8. Beardsley escapes again…
Pedro may have been born in Wallsend but he joined United from Vancouver. The club let him escape again in 1987, allowing Liverpool to buy him for £1.9m, only a year after he'd been Gary Lineker's chief supplier and partner in England's 1986 World Cup campaign. At the time, Pedro's move seemed a fluke – but when Waddle and Gazza followed him out of the door, a pattern emerged. It would take a second coming of the Geordie Messiah to save the club.

9. Mark Lawrenson's fatal sprint
Outpacing Kevin Keegan to a ball in a 1984 FA Cup tie, Mark Lawrenson convinces the Mighty Atom his best days are over. At the end of the season, Keegan hangs up his boots on his 33rd birthday. If he'd lasted another year, with his inspirational presence, could he have helped stave off the decline of the late 1980s?

10. Johnny Giles fractures a leg
The Leeds midfielder's tackle is bad news for George Dalton who, after this Division Two game in January 1964, never plays for United again. In the emergency, Frank Clark becomes central to the defence that will win the Inter-Cities Fairs Cup.

11. Captain John Hope founds a rifle volunteer corps in Edinburgh
Keen to turn the young men of Edinburgh away from drinking and smoking and towards religion, Hope launches a corps of rifle volunteers. Members of this corps make up most of the crowd for the first game of football played in Edinburgh, late in 1873. Impressed, the volunteers buy their own football and, in the local British League of Abstainers office, set up a football club. One of the club's members was Frank Watt, who played for the team and acted as club secretary, starting a career in football administration which led him south of the border in 1895 to make Newcastle United into a trophy winning club. Watt's achievement is all the more astonishing because, not long before his arrival on Tyneside, the club directors had been so appalled by local apathy towards football, they issued a statement saying: "The people of Tyneside do not deserve a professional football club".

> "MAE, WE'RE GOING TO HAVE TO BUY ANDY COLE AND YOU'RE GOING TO HAVE TO FUND THIS ONE"

COCKNEY GEORDIES

Londoners united in black and white – not including Paul 'Sparrow' Moran...

Warren Barton 1995-2002
Dave Beasant 1988-89
Ivan Broadis 1953-55
Les Ferdinand 1995-97
Paul Goddard 1986-88
Bryan Harvey 1958-61
Shaka Hislop 1995-98
Rob Lee 1992-2002
Malcolm Macdonald 1971-76
Kenny Sansom 1988-1989
Imre Varadi 1981-1983

CROWD PLEASERS

11 massive home crowds at St James' Park

1. 68,386 3 September 1930
This is United's record home gate – the fans turning up to see their idol, Hughie Gallacher, return to St James' Park in Chelsea colours.

2. 67,211 19 March 1927
The box-office pull of Gallacher, who scored the only goal, and a Tyne and Wear derby.

3. 66,275 9 March 1929
A seven-goal thriller of a Tyne and Wear derby, which United win by the odd goal.

4. 65,798 26 October 1946
A massive crowd for a league game against Manchester City, rewarded with two points and a Charlie Wayman hat-trick.

5. 63,665 26 December 1951
The crowd had their appetite whetted by Newcastle's 4-1 rout of Sunderland just the day before – but this derby finished 2-2.

6. 63,486 1 March 1930
The fans cheer on United in the FA Cup sixth round but they only draw 1-1 with Hull.

11. CHAMPIONS

Jimmy Lawrence

Billy McCracken   Jack Carr

Dave Willis   Colin Veitch   Peter McWilliam

Jackie Rutherford   Andrew Anderson
Jimmy Howie   Jimmy Stewart
Stanley Allan

The team that beat Blackburn 4-2 on 24 April 1909 to secure the title in an eventful season in which Newcastle set a new points record and lost 9-1 to Sunderland

7. 63,000 24 February 1951
Bristol Rovers almost snatched this FA Cup quarter-final. United won the replay 3-1.

8. 62,873 18 January 1947
Len Shackleton got the only goal of this league game against Spurs.

9. 62,500 15 April 1927
Gallacher packs 'em in again – against Huddersfield in the league.

10. 59,960 16 April 1965
Fans packed in to St James' Park on Good Friday in the spring of 1965 to watch Joe Harvey's side win 2-0 and all but clinch their return to Division One as champions.

11. 59,303 21 May 1969
The second leg of the Inter-Cities Fairs Cup final against Rangers. This gate was 79 higher than the official tally for the first leg of the final eight days later but fans say they were at least 60,000 in the ground against Ujpesti Dozsa.

CULT HEROES

Loved on the Gallowgate

1. The Geordie Dancer
"He's Geordie, he dances" says a fan page on the Internet. Says it almost all – he's Geordie, and he dances in a local pub before every home game.

2. Brian Kilcline
He looked like a Viking raider and often played like one but Killer was the defender whose tenacity and composure helped Newcastle avoid the drop in 1991/92. Once lost his flowing locks while asleep on a sun-bed on a tour of Cyprus. He woke up to find one of his team-mates had cut all his hair off. No one dared own up.

3. Micky Quinn
A wholehearted, well-rounded legend who'd risk physical injury to score a goal and whose nickname – The Mighty Quinn – inspired a decent Newcastle fanzine.

4. Tony Green
Joe Harvey was heartbroken when Tony quit with a damaged knee when he was 25. "He was my very best buy," said Harvey. "I could watch him play all day every day."

5. Tino Asprilla Mad, gifted and adored.

6. Lee Clark
Spotted wearing a T-shirt taking the mickey out of Sunderland while on their books.

7. Temuri Ketsbaia
A hoarding-kicking Georgian wild boy, probably the only player in recent memory to celebrate a goal with more passion than the fans.

8. Terry Hibbitt
Dazzling winger whose name is still sung at St James' Park occasionally, a quarter of a century after he stopped playing for the club.

9. Hughie Gallacher
Convivial, gifted, with the dress sense of an immodest Chicago gangster and the thirst of an alcoholic, Hughie is an icon to those Toon fans who remember him.

10. Philippe Albert
Top 'tache, great chip of Peter Schmeichel, scary runs into the opposition half…

11. Mirandinha

Okay, it didn't work, but the Brazilian scored twice to earn us a point at Old Trafford, shot from anywhere, and kung-fu kicked Dave Beasant once in frustration, running away before the ref noticed. And sold a fair few half-Newcastle, half-Brazil strips.

CULTURAL REVOLUTIONS

How Newcastle United has shaped music, TV, movies…you name it.

1. Purely Belter

This tale of two teenagers dreaming of having their own season ticket for St James' Park is a minor triumph. Alan Shearer has a cameo role and has the mickey taken out of his musical tastes in an exhilarating sequence where the lads nick his sports car. But the Mackems' Stadium Of Light sometimes doubles as St James' Park.

2. "Oz is harder than Yosser!"

A chant which surfaced briefly in Newcastle v Liverpool games when *Auf Wiedersehen, Pet* and *The Boys From The Blackstuff* were on TV in the early 1980s. The matter of which fictional hardman was harder – Oz (Jimmy Nail) or Yosser (Bernard Hughes) has never been satisfactorily resolved. A future *Celebrity Wrestling* fixture?

3. Fog On The Tyne

Chris Waddle said of this record by his old mate: "I like the Lindisfarne version but Gazza's was rubbish. He gave me a signed copy but I melted it down on the bonfire."

4. "Chelsea represent everything I detest"

In one episode of *Whatever Happened To The Likely Lads?*, Terry (James Bolam) tells a new acquaintance who supports Chelsea, not Newcastle: "Chelsea represent everything I detest in football." The joke is even funnier because Bolam's co-star Rodney Bewes was a Chelsea fan.

THE SCOUT'S REPORT ON FRANK CLARK SAID: "HE'S NOT THAT SKILFUL, DOESN'T LIKE RECEIVING THE BALL"

5. "Ten out of ten and one for neatness"

Twelve years after intoning "They think it's all over", Kenneth Wolstenholme was commentating on the Tyne Tees regional football show, *Shoot!* He was so inspired by a 4-2 away win by Middlesbrough at Newcastle that, as striker Stan Cummins scored Boro's fourth, he cried: "That gives him ten out of ten and one for neatness."

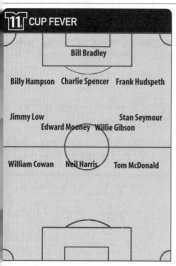

The 11 that won Newcastle's first FA Cup on 27 April 1924

The 11 that lost to Hereford in the FA Cup replay on 5 February 1972

6. Own goal?

Can it be a coincidence that 2004/05 saw enough intrigue, violence and scandal at the club to fill a Hollywood movie when a Hollywood movie is being filmed at the club? The movie, *Goal!* – note the thoughtful use of the exclamation mark to signify enthusiasm – is sponsored by FIFA. The film is – the irony here is so delicious you could almost eat it – a bid to promote the game's image.

7. Jossy's Giants

Joswell 'Jossy' Blair was a brilliant child footballer whose Newcastle United career was curtailed by injury. So, in this kiddie comedy TV series scripted by darts commentator Sid Waddell, he consoles himself by coaching a side called the Glipton Grasshoppers. *Jossy's Giants* T-shirts are still relatively fashionable.

8. Sunday Night at the London Palladium

Just 24 hours after winning the FA Cup in 1955, Newcastle players dropped in to watch this variety show and joined the cast for the all-singing, all-dancing finale.

9. Spender and the missing striker
Ian La Frenais co-wrote *Spender* with St James' Park regular Jimmy Nail, who also plays the titular hero. In one episode, sleuth Spender has to find former Newcastle United striker Kenny Cooper, who has vamoosed. A mooted instalment in which he searched for Stephane Guivarc'h was canned.

10 ."Is Kenny Dalglish a big girl's blouse?"
The furore over Newcastle's 1998 FA Cup tie against Stevenage Borough, prompted *Newsnight*'s Jeremy Paxman to chip in with this question.

11. Sgt Pepper's Lonely Hearts Club Band
Newcastle United's wartime hat-trick hero Albert Stubbins graced the cover.

DEFENSIVE ROCKS
Yes, there have been 11 of them

1. Frank Brennan 349 appearances 1946-1956
Known as The Rock Of Tyneside, almost as if it was his official title, Brennan was a towering, tough-tackling Scottish central defender who was worshipped by the crowd in the decade he spent at St James' Park. One incident in the 1951 FA Cup semi-final against Wolves sums up his devotion to the cause. Rising to head a corner away, he landed badly, stumbled off the pitch, cracked his head against a stacked pipe so hard the whole ground could hear it, but returned to the field still partly concussed and immediately blocked a fierce shot with his head. While his team-mates looked on in astonishment, he blinked, shook his head and smiled.

2. Bob Moncur 358 appearances 1960-1974
Bobby, a dominant centre-half for eight seasons, is truly worshipped for scoring three goals over the two legs of the 1969 Inter-Cities Fairs Cup final as skipper. He was, said his manager Joe Harvey, "the supreme sweeper".

3. **Frank Hudspeth** 482 appearances 1910-1929

At left-back, he was, the *Topical Times* noted, "the type that never gives his manager a moment of anxiety." With Bill McCracken, he was part of the meanest defence in United history – they shipped just 39 goals in 42 games in Division One in 1919/20.

4. **Frank Clark** 456 appearances 1962-1975

Signed despite a scout's report which noted: "He's not that skilful, he doesn't like receiving the ball and he can't wait to get rid of it", no one has played more games for United since World War 2 than Clark. He won the Inter-Cities Fairs Cup with Newcastle but, after a daft free transfer, enjoyed greater glory with Brian Clough.

5. **Bill McCracken** 444 appearances 1904-1923

A wily defender, McCracken was so good at stepping up to leave attackers offside that the FA changed the rules so a player was offside if he was nearer the goal than the last defender (hitherto he was off if he was closer than two defenders). With his usual timing, McCracken retired the summer before the rule was introduced. An astute tactical reader of the game, he could handle even the most gifted strikers.

6. **Bobby Cowell** 327 appearances 1943-1956

"Totally dedicated, a man who literally cried with frustration if we lost," was how Jackie Milburn summed up full-back Bobby Cowell. He monopolised the right-back position for almost a decade, winning three FA Cup finals (clearing off the line in one of them) and could have gone on for longer but for injury.

7. **Peter McWilliam** 240 appearances 1902-1911

A crisp, precise passer of the ball, whose reading of the game was so good he hardly needed to tackle, this Scottish attacking defender would, 80 years later, have suited Keegan's Entertainers.

8. **David Craig** 429 appearances 1960-1978

As essential at right-back as Clark at left-back, Craig is the only player to have featured in both the Magpies' early European adventures: 1968-1971 and 1977/78. His consistent stylish contribution in defence and his flair going forward was much missed, through injury, in the 1974 FA Cup final and the 1976 League Cup final.

9. **Alf McMichael** 433 appearances 1949-1963

A cracking signing from Linfield, McMichael was, in the words of Stanley Matthews, "One of the best left-backs I ever played against." McMichael won 40 caps for Northern Ireland, playing in the 1958 World Cup. Such a favourite with fans, they forgave him his own goal after 32 seconds against West Bromwich Albion in 1951.

10. John Anderson 316 appearances 1982-1992
Possibly the only favour Gordon Lee ever did United was giving this versatile, committed, defender a free transfer to St James' Park while he was managing Preston. He didn't miss a match when Newcastle won promotion back to Division One in 1983/84. Not blessed with silky skills, Anderson was a totemic player for fans at a time when the club was struggling, his devotion to the cause never in doubt.

11. Philippe Albert 123 appearances 1994-1999
The Belgian fitted perfectly into Keegan's team. He loved to attack. Many of United's most fluent moves started with him in possession. Sometimes caught out of position, but tougher and more effective as a stopper than often given credit for.

DIDN'T WE HAVE A LOVELY TIME THE DAY WE…

11 awful away trips

1. Oxford United 5 Newcastle 2 February 1992
As Michael Bolam notes in his book The Magpies: "The bottom had been reached and the final whistle wasn't greeted with any catcalls or jeering from the travelling fans, just numb silence." At least the mist gave fans an excuse not to watch.

2. Chelsea 2 Newcastle 1 November 1981
Just the four away fans coaches attacked by Chelsea's stylish fans.

3. Plymouth Argyle 2 Newcastle 0 December 1991
Losing to rubbish, having to stand on the open terrace in pouring rain on a Friday night kick-off… the very definition of Toon masochism.

4. Manchester United 4 Newcastle 0 August 1996
No mercy in the Charity Shield from Fergie's Fledglings, the weather – fans got soaked in a cloudburst as they left Wembley – or from the Department of Transport who had helpfully ensured there were roadworks all along the A1.

5. Portsmouth 3 Newcastle 1 October 1991
Driving rain fiercest in the away fans end, Darren Bradshaw sent off, a Micky Quinn goal disallowed, Quinn scores again and crashes into the post. Oh misery, misery!

6. Monaco 3 Newcastle 0 March 1997
The only highlight of this game was the away fans' chorus of "In your Monaco slums".

7. Leeds United 1 Newcastle 0 December 1989
The 900 away fans were pelted with coins and rocks and Vinnie Jones decided to climb over the fence and wind up the home fans to even greater heights.

8. Barcelona 1 Newcastle 0 November 1997
Soaked but still singing, despite a wretched performance and United's strange failure to acknowledge their fans' presence.

9. Aston Villa 3 Newcastle 1 January 1989
Away fans are warned by West Midlands police: "Raising your hands above your head will result in ejection." Mirandinha scores a penalty. Nowt else to cheer about.

10. Swindon Town 2 Newcastle 1 November 1991
The score flatters United; police get over-excited about a conga on the away terrace.

11. Berwick Rangers 0 Newcastle 3 July 1993
Shielfield Park was a great place to go on a windy day for a pre-season friendly if you like having sand and cinders blown in your eyes from the speedway track.

DODGY IMPORTS

Not worth the air fare, work permit, taxi to pick them up at the airport...

1. Marcelino
Or to give him his proper title Elena Sierra Marcelino. Was signed by Ruud Gullit from Real Mallorca in the summer of 1999 for £5.3m. By January 2003 the Spanish defender had still only started 15 league games for United. Chairman Freddy Shepherd put everyone out of their misery by buying out what was left of his contract. Marcelino gave an insight into what to expect when he was injured in his first game against Aston Villa and did not appear after the interval. When he left he said: "The fans called me a thieving Spaniard and a gypsy who robbed the club."

> MARCELINO MOANED: "THE FANS CALLED ME A THIEVING SPANIARD AND A GYPSY WHO ROBBED THE CLUB"

2. Fumaca
Nobody knows where he came from or where he went. But Newcastle fans do know that Fumaca is probably the worst footballer Brazil has ever produced. At least he didn't cost a penny.

3. Stephane Guivarc'h

Guivarc'h was in the squad for the World Cup finals played in his own country and Dalglish assumed that should France win the trophy, then the player's value would soar. He was half-right: France did win the World Cup.

4. Didier Domi

When Ruud Gullit signed Domi from Paris St Germain for £4m in December 1998 Newcastle fans thought Christmas had come early as the French left-back looked tidy enough. But Domi found it hard to settle on Tyneside. He returned to Paris over Christmas 2000 to have Christmas dinner with his mother, never came back, effectively going AWOL. Chairman Freddy Shepherd had to sell him back to Paris St Germain.

5. Alessandro Pistone

> CORDONE TOOK PHOTOS OF AWAY GROUNDS NEWCASTLE VISITED – GROUNDS HE DIDN'T PLAY ON

The left-back was the Italian Under-21 captain when Kenny Dalglish brought him to St James' Park for £4.5m in 1997. But Pistone spent more time on the treatment table than on the pitch. At the players' Christmas party, Pistone was presented with a sheep's heart. This was the same party at which Didi Hamann was given a copy of *Mein Kampf*. Unsubtle even by Basil Fawlty's standards.

6. Silvio Maric

When Ruud Gullit signed Silvio Maric from Croatia Zagreb in February 1999 for £3.75m, the striker had a huge reputation. When the deal threatened to collapse, Newcastle had a plane waiting on the tarmac of their local airport ready to fly to Croatia to fetch Maric. But his Newcastle career never took off. After 12 Premiership starts – and no goals – Sir Bobby Robson sold him to Porto in 2000 for £2m.

7. Andreas Andersson

When Kenny Dalglish wanted a partner for Alan Shearer in 1997 he paid AC Milan £3.5m for Swedish striker Andreas Andersson. Before he put pen to paper at St James' Park, Dalglish took the Swede out to lunch with Shearer, but goals were not on Andersson's menu and he was shipped back to Sweden with AIK Stockholm.

8. Lionel Perez

When Newcastle fans heard they had signed Perez they all thought it was Robert Pires, the goal-scoring winger from Metz. Alas, no. Signed in the summer of 1998/99, by March 2000 Perez was still waiting to make his debut for Newcastle. He picked up £500,000 in wages before he was sent to Cambridge United on loan.

9. Daniel Cordone

The Argentinian striker had a disastrous time at St James' Park. To be fair he only cost £500,000 on a season's loan from Racing Club Argentina in the summer of 2000 and got off to a good start when he scored in his first game the pre-season friendly against Washington DC United. But he only made 12 starts and scored just two goals. Before he left Cordone started taking photos of all the away grounds Newcastle played on. But he didn't get to play on many himself.

10. John Karelse

Ruud Gullit paid NAC Breda £750,000 for fellow-Dutchman Karelse – just a week before he walked out of the door at St James' Park. But Sir Bobby Robson did not rate the keeper. Karelse only started three games for Newcastle – one of them a goalless draw against Arsenal at Highbury – and returned to Holland on a free transfer.

11. Diego Gavilan

The young midfielder became the first Paraguayan to play in the Premiership when he joined Newcastle from Cerro Porteno for £2.5m in January 2000. But the player dubbed Sparrowhawk had his wings clipped at St James' Park. He was sent to Mexico on loan to Autonoma de Guadelajara. A flop at Newcastle, he played for Paraguay in the 2002 World Cup finals.

DON'T STAND SO CLOSE TO ME

11 frankly paltry attendances at St James' Park. Spread out a bit lads.

1. 3,000 4 April 1973

Rumour has it that so few fans turned up because, when told Como would be playing St James' Park, they assumed people meant Perry Como. Proof that the phrase "cup fever" did not extend to the Anglo-Italian Cup.

2. 4,609 16 December 1992

Nineteen years after Como, the Anglo-Italian Cup returns to Newcastle with the same effect. To be fair, Cesena were never the sexiest team in Italian football.

3. 6,167 29 November 1989

The romance of the Full Members Cup – and Oldham Athletic.

4. 6,345 22 September 1962

Division Two, Norwich City, early season optimism waning…

5. 6,843 11 August 1981
Not many fans could be bothered to watch West Bromwich Albion in a friendly.

6. 7,134 8 May 1979
Division Two ennui and Wrexham arrive…

7. 7,500 August 1979
Sparta Rotterdam didn't set the pulses racing at a pre-season friendly.

8. 7,754 6 August 1966
Nobody knew where Aalborg was.

9. 7,986 26 April 1978
After a 3-0 drubbing by QPR, fans vote with their feet as Norwich City roll into town.

10. 8,568 8 August 1992
The start of the Exhibition Super Challenge tournament and the fixture computer – or flunkie with bits of paper in a hat – has decided that Newcastle should make an exhibition of themselves facing the super challenge of, er, Middlesbrough.

11. 9,073 27 August 1980
The magic of the League Cup second round against Bury.

ELEVEN IN A ROW

A glorious start to 1992/93:, 11 wins in a row on the way to promotion to Premiership

1. Southend United H 3-2
2. Derby County A 2-1
3. West Ham United H 2-0
4. Luton Town H 2-0
5. Bristol Rovers A 2-1
6. Portsmouth H 3-1
7. Bristol City H 5-0
8. Peterborough United A 1-0
9. Brentford H 2-1
10. Tranmere Rovers H 1-0
11. Sunderland A 2-1
Then Grimsby spoilt the party.

EUROPEAN TOP SCORERS

A bit embarrassing really

1. Alan Shearer 28
2. Craig Bellamy 11
3. Shola Ameobi 10
   Wyn Davies 10
5. Tino Asprilla 9
   Bryan Robson 9
7. Nobby Solano 7
8. Patrick Kluivert 5
   Laurent Robert 5
   Jimmy Scott 5
   Gary Speed 5
   Tommy Gibbs 5

11 EUROPEAN GLORY

Willie McFaul

David Craig   Frank Clark
Bobby Moncur Ollie Burton

Jim Scott Preben Arentoft Tommy Gibb

Bryan Robson Wyn Davies Jack Sinclair

The 11 who won United's only European trophy: line up in the second leg of the 1969 Inter-Cities Fairs Cup final against Ujpesti Dozsa

EUROVISIONS

Nights of continental celebration

1. 17 September 1997 Glorious as Asprilla's hat-trick against Barcelona was, it's easy to forget that United only just held on in the last two minutes, as Barça fought back to 2-3. An astonishing Champions League debut.

2. 15 June 1969 Newcastle, 2-0 down at half-time and looking doomed, grab three goals to win their first and only European trophy. A performance of pure heroism against Ujpesti Dozsa in the 1969 Inter-Cities Fairs Cup final which surpasses even the thrill of winning 3-0 on home soil in the first leg.

3. 13 September 1994 Royal Antwerp are played off their park in the UEFA Cup, losing 5-0.

4. 13 November 2002 Feyenoord have been good to United. A 4-0 drubbing of the Dutch side kicked off Newcastle's triumphant European campaign in 1968/69 and this 3-2 victory, earned when Craig Bellamy punishes a keeper's fumble from a Kieron Dyer shot, makes United the first team to qualify for the second stage of the Champions League after losing their first three games.

5. 21 May 1969 Rangers fans may have caused havoc, but this 2-0 victory in the Inter-Cities Fairs Cup semi-final is still deeply satisfying. A hammered volley by Jackie Sinclair seals United's place the final.

6. 30 September 1970 This 2-0 demolition of Inter is often forgotten because the 1970/71 Fairs Cup campaign petered out. But this game has everything: a headed goal from Bobby Moncur, a brawl in which the referee is punched by the Inter keeper Vieri and, after coming round, sends the keeper off – a decision which sparks another brawl. A 3-1 aggregate win over the Italian giants was some result.

7. 27 September 1994 Antwerp may have expected United to go through the motions after being stuffed in the first leg of this UEFA Cup tie but Andy Cole, playing despite suffering from shin splints, bags a hat-trick as United won 5-2. For some, the highlight is a superb dribble by Scott Sellars which helps Cole complete a hat-trick.

8. 11 September 1968 "Score and score well, we need a three-goal lead to take to Feyenoord" – those are the instructions from manager Joe Harvey. United duly oblige, winning 4-0 with winger Geoff Allen tormenting the Dutch defence.

9. 3 December 1996 Not a great game (Newcastle limp past Metz 2-0) but a great celebration from Asprilla as he hoists his shirt on a corner flag and is booked.

10. 2 May 1973 Not entirely to be taken seriously, the Anglo-Italian Cup has given United fans the odd treat. Sadly, only 9,500 fans were at St James' Park to watch Torino get hammered 5-1 in a game where the goal tally was almost matched by the number of players sent off (four).

11. 11 May 1997. This 5-0 thrashing of Nottingham Forest clinched United's first Champions League place.

EXILES

Geordie stars who could have started at United

Jack Allen
Peter Beardsley
Michael Carrick
Bobby Charlton
Jack Charlton
Don Hutchison
Stan Mortensen
Jimmy Mullen
Bobby Robson
Alan Shearer
Dennis Tueart

> HARVEY SAID: "SCORE AND SCORE WELL. WE NEED A THREE GOAL LEAD TO TAKE TO FEYENOORD"

FANS WHO BECAME PLAYERS

Usually to good effect

Jack Allen
Joe Allon
Charlie Crowe
Lee Clark
Robbie Elliott
Paul Gascoigne
Kevin Keegan
Tony Lormor
Alan Shearer
Paul Stephenson
Alan Thompson

FOOTBALLING FIRSTS

Records, statistical achievements, set by the club and its players

1. First club to lose first three games in a Champions League group and still qualify for the next phase – in 2002.
2. First player to score 200 goals in the Premiership. If you're going to score that many, you don't want to put too much effort into your celebrations, do you Alan?
3. First team to appear in nine FA Cup finals – a feat United managed back in 1952.
4. First club to record an average home gate of 56,299 – this record, which stood for many years, was achieved when United won promotion back to the old Division One in 1947/48.
5. First top-flight English club to play a Brazilian. They're all the rage these days but when Mirandinha made his debut wearing the famous No9 shirt in September 1987, the transfer was a real shot in the dark.

6. First player to score five goals in an England shirt – Supermac's feat, against Cyprus in 1975, has still not been matched.

7. First club to pay a £7,000 transfer fee. Officially, Newcastle paid £6,500 for Hughie Gallacher in 1925, but club historian Paul Joannou noted that the *Newcastle Chronicle* claimed "£7000 is the generally accepted sum". This would have been a British transfer record.

8. First Newcastle No9 to score 42 goals against Middlesbrough. In seven seasons, Albert Stubbins scored three goals or more in a game on eight different occasions against the Boro.

9. First ever away win over Southampton in the Premiership. United just managed to notch up their first Premiership victory over the Saints in September 2004.

10. First ever team to win four Wembley finals. Newcastle achieved this against Arsenal in 1952, winning the FA Cup.

11. First club to win the FA Cup six times in the 20th century – thanks to an inspired performance by Jimmie Scoular in the 1955 final against Manchester City.

THE FRENCH CONNECTION

They have usually failed to cut le moutard

1. David Ginola

Because he was worth it. At the time, he said he loved playing for Newcastle because "All the people want me here, they look me in the eye and say 'David, I want to play with you.'" Later, in a fit of tristesse induced by too many ads for hair products, coffee, etc, he claimed signing for Newcastle was "the worst mistake I ever made".

2. Laurent Robert

Like many French football exports, Robert isn't from France but from Reunion in the Indian Ocean. A mystery, riddle and enigma, he bid adieu by stripping on the pitch.

3. Olivier Bernard

A real bargain – a free signing from Lyon – and a decent left-back whose service was marred by misquotes in a tabloid that he found the north-east grey and boring.

4. Jean-Alain Boumsong

£8m is a lot of money but give him time.

5. Charles N'Zogbia

The 18-year-old midfielder has already prompted the headline "Zog on the Tyne".

6. Sylvain Distin
A loan signing from PSG who demanded a rumoured £25,000 a week to stay on.

7. Alain Goma
Injured at Newcastle, desperate to leave, he shone in Fulham's defence, attributing his poor form at St James' Park to the fact that "Newcastle didn't work hard enough".

8. Laurent Charvet
The fruit of Kenny's unwise cross-channel shopping spree in the summer of 1998.

9. Lionel Perez
After conceding four goals and seven penalties for Sunderland in the 1997/98 promotion play off, Perez joined Newcastle's goalkeeping staff. Never played competitively for the club and later claimed he "had lost his football" on Tyneside.

10. Stephane Guivarc'h
Billed as the French Alan Shearer. Wasn't even the French Duncan Shearer.

11. David Terrier
Didn't play for West Ham and didn't even make the bench at Newcastle in 1998.

FROM THE TYNE TO THE WEAR...
Or the other way around: 11 players who've crossed the great divide

1. Bob Stokoe
A converted half-back who started out as a centre-forward, Stokoe won the FA Cup as a player in 1955 with Newcastle United and, more famously, with Sunderland in 1973. Linked with the job many times, Stokoe never actually managed Newcastle.

2. John Auld
Centre-half in Sunderland's Team Of All The Talent, Auld was the first player to transfer from the Wear to the Tyne. He joined United as an amateur in 1896, so the Mackems got no fee; this led to what one hack called "childish hubbub" on Wearside.

3. Len Shackleton
The clown prince of soccer entertained on the Tyne and the Wear. The Rokermen got the best of him. He never really got on with Newcastle's management and, after 29 goals in 64 games, joined Sunderland where he spent the next ten years.

11. FIRST EVER
NEWCASTLE UNITED TEAM

Andrew Ramsay

Harry Jeffery   James Miller

J. Bowman   Joe McKane
   Bobby Creilly   Willie Graham

Tom Crate   Joseph Wallace
   Willie Thompson   Jock Sorley

They drew 2-2 away against Woolwich Arsenal on 2 September 1893

4. Barry Venison

Now more famous for his unique personal style than his ability, Barry Venison captained the Rokermen when he was only 20. Joining Newcastle in 1992, he forced his way into the England side, skippered United and was generally inspirational.

5. Stanley Anderson

A stylish central defender, Anderson was a legend at Roker Park but, after 14 years, stunned Wearside by joining Joe Harvey's Newcastle. An astute short-term buy, he helped Newcastle climb back up the league, winning the old Division Two in 1965.

6. Bryan 'Pop' Robson

The striker won the Inter-Cities Fairs Cup with Newcastle, scored 97 goals in black and white, and later served Sunderland – in five separate spells – as a player and coach.

7. Lee Clark

Inconsistent but gifted, Lee Clark left Newcastle for Sunderland to get first-team football. After helping Sunderland win promotion in 1999, he was spotted wearing a t-shirt with the logo "Sad Mackem bastards". He decided he couldn't play for the Mackems against Newcastle at St James' Park. Luckily, Fulham beckoned.

8. Alan Kennedy

Born in Sunderland, Alan Kennedy won two European Cups with Liverpool, but was discovered by Newcastle, spent seven years with the club before joining the Reds and later spent a season with Sunderland.

9. Tom Urwin

The outside-right was at Newcastle Central station on his way to meet Manchester United when he was spotted – and sidetracked – by Bill McCracken in 1924. After six years at United, he served Sunderland as a player and as youth trainer.

10. Tom Rowlandson

In 1905/06, this Edwardian gent with a Lord Kitchener moustache kept goal once for Newcastle as an amateur and later played 12 games for the Wearsiders.

11. Jackie Milburn

Guested for Sunderland in World War 2, but fans never really held it against him.

G IS FOR GEORDIE

11 variations on the theme of Geordie pride

1. "We're like the Basques. We are fighting for a nation. The Geordie nation. Football is about tribalism and we are the Mohicans"

Sir John Hall waxes patriotic about the Geordies. If the Geordies really are the Mohicans they disappeared with James Fenimore Cooper.

2. "The Geordie nation – that's what we're fighting for! London's the enemy – you exploit us. You use us"

A rousing speech from Sir John Hall. Rousing, but daft.

3. "My eventual dream is to have 11 Geordies playing for Newcastle United and 11 in the reserves"
Sir John had this dream in 1994. Ten years later, the squad has players from France, Senegal, Portugal, Holland, Cameroon, Nigeria and Canning Town.

4. "We're already bigger and more financially stable than Barcelona"
Douglas Hall says Newcastle are bigger than those trophy-rich Catalan upstarts.

5. "The Geordies are a resilient race"
Jackie Milburn noting the immediate optimism which surged through Tyneside after the signing of Micky Quinn and Mark McGhee in the summer of 1989.

6. "Southern supporters don't have the passion and pride of a Geordie"
Malcolm Macdonald looks back in wonder in his book *Never Afraid To Miss*.

7. "Howay the Lads!"
President Jimmy Carter greets the north-east on a whirlwind tour in May 1977.

8. "I spend more time talking, thinking, anticipating, worrying, rejoicing, despairing and living Newcastle United than anything else in my life"
Independent financial adviser, answering a club questionnaire in 1995.

9. "In God's own country up there, if the team win, it lifts the city"
Jimmy Nail talks Toon in his autobiography.

10. "Here on Teesside we wind up the Mackems, calling them Plastic Geordies"
A Boro fan, pontificating about Geordies. Anything to avoid watching his team.

11. "From Forest Hall to Timbuktu/Every Geordie's proud of you"
The stirring couplet in United's 1974 FA Cup final single, *Howway The Lads*.

GAZZAMANIA!

11 great moments involving the daft Geordie genius while he was at Newcastle

1. Sending Vinnie Jones a rose after the Wimbledon hard man had grabbed Gazza by the balls during a game in February 1988.

2. His arrogantly taken penalty against Swindon Town in the FA Cup. Gazza, knowing England manager Bobby Robson was watching, inspired Newcastle to a 5-0 thrashing of Swindon, scoring twice, in the 1987/88 fourth round tie.

3. Winning the FA Youth Cup almost single-handed. Newcastle weren't expected to win the 1985 FA Youth Cup final after drawing the first leg at home 0-0 against Watford. But Gazza inspired the young Magpies to a 4-1 victory in the second leg at Vicarage Road to lift the trophy for the second time in the club's history.

4. Complaining he was always being hounded for autographs, Gazza was told he should go incognito. After pondering this for second, he asked: "**Where's cognito?**"

5. Losing Kevin Keegan's boots. Impressed to be asked to clean the star's boots, he decided to show them to his mates but lost them on the Metro on the way home.

6. Paying **£20 for a Mars bar** in a shop in his hometown of Dunston – and telling the shop owner to buy sweets for the local kids with the change.

7. His double handshake with Mirandinha. He was so keen to make the Brazilian striker feel at home he stood first in line to shake Mirandinha's hand and ran to the back of the line-up to shake his hand again. Gazza even named his goldfish Mirandinha. But he drew the line at passing to him.

8. Trying to impress then Newcastle boss Jack Charlton by buying fishing gear and asking for **angling lessons.** Big Jack chucked the new rods in the river, poured some Newcastle Brown Ale into the water, dipped his fishing rod in and caught a whopper.

9. Promising to score in a 1987 Littlewoods Cup tie against Blackpool to **atone for an error** which had led to a goal in the first leg – and doing just that. Newcastle won the game 4-1 and the second round tie 4-2 on aggregate.

> PAYING £20 FOR A MARS BAR, GAZZA TOLD THE SHOP OWNER TO BUY SWEETS FOR THE KIDS WITH THE CHANGE

10. Showing his stomach to Chelsea fans at Stamford Bridge in 1987 – his way of reprimanding the home fans for chanting "**Fatty!**" as he ran out onto the pitch.

11. Interviewed in March 2002 by the *Guardian*, Dino Zoff was asked what he thought of Gazza's idea that he might manage Lazio. Zoff's response: "**Gascoigne, manager Lazio** hahaha. Gascoigne, manager Lazio, hahahahaha. Gascoigne, manager Lazio, hahahaha. Now I have heard it all. Thank you for telling me that. Thank you."

GENIUS ENVY

Players who've graced St James' Park but not for the right team

1. Eddie Hapgood
A Gooner but a great defender, who played in the England side that tonked Norway 4-0 at St James' Park in 1938. Once scored a penalty with his head, a Tinoesque feat.

2. Gianluigi Buffon
When Juve came to St James' Park in the 2002/03 Champions League, he had the Tyne Bridge embroidered on his gloves. And he made some cracking saves.

3. Christian Vieri
Sulky, beefy Inter striker, a Newcastle No9 in the wrong country and wrong league.

4. Gheorghe Hagi
Tricksy midfield maestro, looked good even in quiet games in Newcastle in Euro 96.

5. Stanley Matthews
Also starred for England v Norway in 1938. The greatest winger United never had.

6. Joe Mercer
A stylish maestro who starred at St James' Park in a wartime international .

7. Johnny Rep
Dutch master who helped Bastia blow United away In the 1977/78 UEFA Cup.

8. Andriy Shevchenko
Didn't get much chance to shine at St James' Park for Ukraine against England in the summer of 2004, but he's a risk the fans would dearly love the club to take.

9. Peter Shilton
The keeper Supermac feared the most.

10. Hristo Stoichkov
Scored one superb goal after three minutes against Romania at St James' Park in Euro 96 and went to sleep. Fans still recall the goal.

11. Cliff Jones
Scored a hat-trick for Spurs at St James' Park in a 5-2 thrashing in August 1959. If he'd flown down the wing for Newcastle, the early 1960s might have been less grim.

GET HIM OFF!

11 players who have been booed at St James' Park

1. Wayne Fereday
Arguably the most inconsistent winger Newcastle have ever had. He only played 32 games in 1989/90 but is still the subject of a rant on *www.nufc.com* which begins: "Quite simply, he was a bottler. A big wet tart of a bottler, who could gallop with gay abandon down the wing like a Shetland pony on acid, provided: a) he didn't take the ball with him or b) no big nasty defenders tried to tackle him."

2. Graham Oates
To critics, to quote the Toonarama fansite: "He was a utility player – he could play in any position with equal incompetence". He arrived at St James' Park in 1976 and endeared himself by scoring an own goal from 25-yards out on his full home debut.

3. Tommy Gibb
You might have thought that if Gibb was good enough to play 171 consecutive games, the Gallowgate might give him some credit. But the abuse got so bad he threatened to quit. Manager Joe Harvey even suggested he only play in away games. He stuck it out for seven years but, in 1975, joined Sunderland on a free.

4. Ronald Orr
Inside-forward barracked out of the club by fans in 1908, gratefully fleeing to join Liverpool after seven years of abuse and decent performances.

5. William Cowan
An elegant, gifted inside-forward, he began to lose form in 1924/25 and was greeted with such vitriol by home fans he was quoted as saying:"I'd rather drop into minor football than remain here." He left to join Manchester City.

6. Bill Paterson
Stylish rather than physically commanding, this Scottish centre-half had the bad luck to be asked to replace crowd favourite Frank Brennan who was in dispute with the club, in 1954. Barracked, jeered, abused, he admitted:"I appeared a misfit" and, in 1958, joined Rangers, where he reached the Cup Winners' Cup final.

7. Mike Hooper
Super Hooper to Super Blooper took the Bristol-born keeper 23 games in 1993/94. Not even Kevin Keegan's threat to resign could stop the booing and hate mail.

8. Steve Hardwick
Promising England youth international keeper whose habit of alternating world class saves with world class gaffes turned the crowd against him in 1977.

9. Charles Burgess
A consistent right-back who left after the 1900/01 season after fans' abuse.

10. Albert Gosnall
Useful winger whose sole offence was to replace the popular Bobby Templeton on the wing in 1904.

11. John Tudor
Looking a bit like the simple-minded country cousin of that *Dead Ringers* bloke John Culshaw, Tudor battled home fans as much as opponents as he strove to replace Bryan 'Pop' Robson in 1976. But, alongside Malcolm Macdonald, he won fans round.

GIVE THAT MAN A GOLD WATCH!
Newcastle players with the most appearances

1. **Jimmy Lawrence** 496
2. **Frank Hudspeth** 472
3. **Frank Clark** 456
4. **Alf McMichael** 433
5. **Bill McCracken** 432
6. **David Craig** 412
7. **Bobby Mitchell** 408
8. **Jackie Milburn** 397
9. **Rob Lee** 380
10. **Will Low** 367
11. **Tom McDonald** 367

These totals exclude wartime games and uncompetitive fixtures.

MIKE HOOPER WENT FROM SUPER HOOPER TO SUPER BLOOPER IN JUST 23 GAMES

GLADLY MISSED

11 things fans don't miss about matchdays of yore

1. Monkey chants greeting black players.
2. New cars being driven around the ground by local garages in a bizarre sales pitch.
3. Being searched for weapons on entry to the Gallowgate.
4. Millwall fans.
5. The St James' Park wind tunnel effect.
6. Running for the bus as full-time approached.
7. Pre-match speculation about useless utility players we were going to sign.
8. The Leazes End when it cost 45p and the man on the gate never had change.
9. Getting crushed on the way out.
10. The barmaid at the Haymarket Hotel who poked you with a window pole if you made too much noise.
11. National Front paper sellers outside the Gallowgate End.
This selection was culled from the survey of fans on *www.nufc.com*.

GOALS, GOALS, GOALS!

High-scoring Newcastle games

1. Newcastle 16 Alberta All-Stars 2 1 June 1949
It was a post-season tour but 16 goals against Edmonton's finest is some haul, with Milburn scoring six. Other friendlies are ignored here for entirely subjective reasons.

2. Newcastle 13 Newport County 0 5 October 1946
Even more famous for debutant Len Shackleton's double hat-trick than for the scoreline. This is the only competitive match in which three hat-tricks have been scored by Newcastle players – Charlie Wayman got the other treble.

3. Newcastle 7 Aston Villa 5 10 March 1928
Both sides were adjusting to changes in the offside law. United went 4-0 up after half an hour, Villa fought back to 4-2, before United extended their lead to 7-2. With the Midlanders down to ten men – after their keeper was carried off – and eight minutes to go, the result seemed in no doubt. But Villa, inspired by chicken-rearing striker Pongo Waring, pulled it back to 7-5.

3. Tranmere Rovers 6 Newcastle 6 1 October 1991
At 3-3 after 90 minutes, and level at extra-time in this
Zenith Data Systems tie, Newcastle were so
knackered they couldn't win the penalty shoot-out.

THE ST JAMES' PARK
WIND TUNNEL EFFECT
IS JUST ONE OF THE
THINGS WE DON'T MISS

5. Liverpool 6 Newcastle 5 4 December 1909
Inside-forward Ronald Orr had to leave Newcastle
because of the abuse he received from fans. He
repaid them handsomely in this top flight fixture,
scoring four times for Liverpool as they came back
from 5-2 down to snatch the points.

5. Manchester United 4 Newcastle 7 13 September 1930
The Red Devils were having a hellish time when Newcastle came to Old Trafford.
Bottom of the old Division One – they would be relegated at season's end – they
held their own for an hour, with the score at 4-4, before Newcastle grabbed three
more to show that, though Gallacher was gone, they knew where the net was.

5. Newcastle 4 Portsmouth 7 15 November 1930
Two months after trouncing Manchester United, Newcastle were walloped by the
same scoreline. The result so shocked United, they lost their next game, to the
Mackems at Roker Park, 5-0.

5. Newcastle 9 Liverpool 2 1 January 1934
Seven goals in the last half-hour – the only time the club have scored that many in
the second half of a competitive fixture – sealed this astonishing victory.

5. Chelsea 6 Newcastle 5 10 September 1958
Chelsea scored the winner five minutes from time; United were 5-3 up at one point.

10. Newcastle 1 Sunderland 9 5 December 1908
The consolations for Newcastle fans are: a) this record home defeat is now almost a
century ago and b) United won the title the same season.

11. QPR 5 Newcastle 5 22 September 1984
Four-nil up at half-time, 5-3 ahead after 84 minutes, Newcastle snatched a draw from
the jaws of victory on QPR's plastic pitch. "Absolutely diabolical," said Newcastle
boss Jack Charlton. He had a point.

'GREAT' GAFFERS

If it weren't for the format of this book, we'd have stopped at number 7

1. Joe Harvey
Manager for 13 years from 1962. Won promotion as champions in 1964 and suffered no relegations. Won United's first – and to date only – European trophy, the Inter-Cities Fairs Cup in 1969. Took the club to the FA Cup final of 1974 but saw his side well beaten by Liverpool. He moved upstairs in 1975 and became chief scout. He was involved with the club until his death in 1989.

2. Kevin Keegan
Probably no man has made such a contribution to Newcastle United as Kevin Keegan. An inspirational skipper, he led the club to promotion in 1983/84. But it is as Newcastle manager that Keegan is best remembered. Who will ever forget his side, dubbed The Entertainers? He took the club back into Europe after 17 years in the wilderness and was hailed as The Messiah. But at the start of 1997 he left, following a series of disagreements with the corporate side of the club.

3. Sir Bobby Robson
Didn't win anything in four and a half years at St James' Park but still considered by some as arguably the best manager in the club's history. He built a Newcastle side good enough to challenge for honours. He just missed out on both FA Cup and Premiership success but led Newcastle back into the Champions League. All Tyneside was elated when he was knighted in June 2002 but just over two years later he was sacked, with various justifications made for his rather shabby treatment.

4. Stan Seymour
Like Keegan, he was player and manager at St James' Park. In his time he was known as Mr Newcastle. As first he was a director but gloried in the title honorary manager from 1939-1947 and 1950-54. In that second spell United won the FA Cup twice. In 1955, back on the board, he over-ruled manager Duggie Livingstone, reinstated Jackie Milburn into the FA Cup final team and saw Wor Jackie head a goal after only 45 seconds as Newcastle beat Manchester City 3-1. Later, he lured Keegan to St James' Park but he also got into all sorts of daft squabbles.

5. Arthur Cox
John The Baptist to Keegan's Geordie Messiah. Hardly anyone had heard of Coxie when he replaced Bill McGarry in 1980 but helped by chairman Stan Seymour and Newcastle Breweries he brought Kevin Keegan to Newcastle. With Keegan, Beardsley and Waddle playing some fine football, Cox won promotion in 1983/84

but quit when refused funds to buy new players. But he had formed a bond with Keegan and came back to work with him when King Kev returned as manager.

6. Andy Cunningham
The first proper manager Newcastle have had, he did a difficult job in clearing out stars like Hughie Gallacher who were setting a poor example to the youngsters, won the FA Cup in 1932 but saw his young side get relegated and quit.

7. Willie McFaul
After great service as player and coach, Irishman Willie McFaul was given the managers job in 1985 when Jack Charlton sensationally walked out after a friendly. McFaul gave Paul Gascoigne his first chance and brought the first Brazilian, Mirandinha, to the English league. McFaul almost had it cracked when, in the summer of 1988, he brought in Andy Thorn, John Hendrie, John Robertson and Dave Beasant but he couldn't replace Gazza, sold to Spurs, and this cost him his job.

8. Kenny Dalglish
United needed a big name to replace Keegan and who better than Kenny Dalglish? Sadly, Dalglish is not remembered with affection on Tyneside mainly because of some bad buys. He did take Newcastle to Wembley for the FA Cup final in 1998 and qualify for the Champions League. And he presided over one of Newcastle's greatest games the 3-2 victory over Barcelona in their first Champions League game in 1997.

9. Ossie Ardiles
The Argentinian World Cup winner found the hot seat at St James' Park too hot as United, in true Ardiles fashion, played fine football but couldn't defend for toffee.

10. Ruud Gullit
As with Dalglish, there was universal approval when Gullit took over from the Scot just a couple of games into the 1998/99 season. As with Dalglish, Gullit took Newcastle to an FA Cup final but, like Dalglish, finished on the losing side. Gullit's man-management let him down at St James' Park. Just ask Alan Shearer, Rob Lee...

11. Gordon Lee
The Midlander is notorious as the Newcastle United manager who got rid of superhero and star striker Malcolm Macdonald. But Lee put together a tidy team which finished fifth in the top flight in his first season. Even with Supermac sold to Arsenal, Newcastle looked to be improving. But Lee quit in January 1977 to take over as manager of Everton. Rumours that he refused to sign Scottish or black players haven't made the Toon regard him any more fondly.

GREAT SCOT

10 players – and one secretary – who crossed the border to become legends

1. Hughie Gallacher

Possibly the greatest centre-forward of all-time, Gallacher scored in 82 per cent of his games for Newcastle. After finishing top goalscorer five seasons in a row, Wee Hughie was sold by the directors who disapproved of his fondness for downing a few before a game, getting banned by referees and punching people. The club got £10,000 for him from Chelsea, even though the player protested: "I have been sold like a slave for a bag of gold." His return with Chelsea prompted a record home gate of 68,386 with 10,000 more locked out in the streets. In 1957, at the age of 54, depressed, he threw himself in front of the York to Edinburgh express train.

2. Bobby Moncur

One of United's best skippers and central defenders, Moncur was the key figure for eight seasons, even scoring – as centre-half – a hat-trick over the two legs of the 1969 Inter-Cities Fairs Cup final against Ujpesti Dozsa. Somehow, Manchester United, Wolves and Preston all missed his talent in trials.

3. Bobby Mitchell

BOBBY MITCHELL CAME TO BE KNOWN AS BOBBY DAZZLER TO TOON FANS

Glaswegian winger who terrorised defences for more than a decade for Newcastle and was known as Bobby Dazzler. Played a vital role in Newcastle's three FA Cup wins in the 1950s, a big game player before the cliché had even been coined.

4. Frank Watt

If any one could be described as Newcastle's answer to Sir Matt Busby it is Watt. Arriving in 1896 as secretary/manager – when the roles were indistinguishable – he steered Newcastle to promotion in 1898. Before he died in 1932, Newcastle had won all four of their league titles and three FA Cups. He had, says Roger Hutchinson in *The Toon*, "a trademark handlebar moustache which would have done credit to a water buffalo," a clear vision of the club's destiny and an easy humorous manner – characteristics too few of his successors in the boardroom have shared.

5. Peter McWilliam

This left-half – known as Peter The Great – from Inveravon was snapped from under Sunderland's nose and helped Newcastle win the league in 1905. Blessed with vision, a body swerve, great passing range and a determination only to tackle if forced to, he enjoyed seven fine seasons before a knee injury wrecked his career. Won the FA Cup as player, with Newcastle in 1910 and as a coach, with Spurs in 1921.

6. Ronnie Simpson
Glaswegian keeper with an astonishing career who won the FA Cup with Newcastle in 1952 and 1955 and, at the age of 37 won the European Cup with Celtic in 1967. An automatic choice for Newcastle in the 1950s, famed for his agility and superb reflexes, he made his league debut for Queens Park Rangers in June 1945 when he was just 14 years and 304 days old.

7. Jimmy Lawrence
Two errors in FA Cup finals blighted a remarkable career for this Glaswegian keeper. A leader in the fledgling players union, Jimmy was valued for his effect on squad morale as much as for his performances. But he was key to Newcastle's first five runs to the FA Cup final – winning in 1910 – and first three league titles.

8. Jimmy Scoular
An imposing midfielder, a controversial captain, accused of favouring other Scottish players, he foiled Manchester City's tactical switch – the Revie Plan in which the future Leeds manager became a withdrawn striker – in the 1955 FA Cup final. A loud talker, he could be subtle on the pitch, striking accurate 40-yard crossfield passes.

9. Andrew Aitken
Half-back and skipper from Ayr who, from 1895 to 1906, inspired Newcastle, leading them to the first title in 1905 and two FA Cup finals, in 1905 and 1906. Team-mate Alex Gardner said:"He may lack physique but for clever headwork and terrier-like persistency, he is hard to beat." He played in every position for United except keeper.

10. Tom McDonald
The perfect link man for Stan Seymour in the 1920s and, later, Hughie Gallacher, he appears in the top ten appearances and goalscoring charts for Newcastle. He later served the club as a steward in the press box.

11. Wilf Low
The Aberdonian centre-half's nickname, The Laughing Cavalier, seems ironic as, from 1909 to 1924, he destroyed the opposition with the robustness of a Roundhead. He roamed in midfield, breaking down – and prompting – attacks. Retiring in 1924, he was assistant trainer and groundsman but died in a road accident in 1933.

GREEN CARD

United stars seduced by the allure of the Clamdiggers, Stings and Jaws

1. Jeremiah Best
Providence Clamdiggers, Fall River Marksmen, Pawtucket Rangers, New Bedford Whalers 1926-1931

2. Peter Withe
Portland Timers 1973-1975

3. Trevor Hockey
San Diego Jaws, Las Vegas Quicksilvers, San Jose Earthquakes 1976-1977

4. Mick Mahoney
Chicago Stings, California Surf, Los Angeles Lazers 1978-1982

5. Ray Hudson
Fort Lauderdale Strikers 1978-1983, later coach of DC United

6. Paul Cannell
Washington Diplomats, Memphis Rogues, Calgary Boomers, Detroit Express 1978-1981

7. Peter Beardsley
Vancouver Whitecaps 1979-1981

8. Alex Cropley
Toronto Blizzard 1980-1981

9. Viv Busby
Tulsa Roughnecks 1980-1981

10. Howard Gayle
Dallas Sidekicks 1984-1986

11. Kenneth Wharton
Winnipeg Furies 1990-1992

GUTTED

Defeats that still make your skin crawl

1. The 1974 FA Cup final

Liverpool 3 Newcastle 0. The scoreline only tells half the story. Manager Joe Harvey said later: "May 4 1974 will haunt me for ever. I feel sick and embarrassed." One explanation for the team's mysterious failure to do the business suggested in zebra-coloured cyberspace is that the club's FA Cup single *Howway The Lads* was recorded by Harry Herring who was, crucially, not from Newcastle but from Sunderland.

2. The 1998 FA Cup final

Not quite as painful as 1974 but bloody close, the gap in class was so immense and Arsenal didn't even need Dennis Bergkamp or Ian Wright to stroll to a 2-0 victory.

3. Scunthorpe United 3 Newcastle 1 1958

Losing to Third Division North opposition 3-1 in the FA Cup fourth round hurt for a side that had won the trophy three years earlier.

4. Sporting Lisbon 4 Newcastle 1 2005

One-nil up on the night, 2-0 up on aggregate, you know the rest.

5. "The worst reverse in the history of the club" 1964

The scoreline from this FA Cup third round tie at St James' Park on 4 January 1964 says it all: Newcastle United 1 Bedford Town 2. Manager Joe Harvey, analysing United's worst result ever, said: "In football, it's a very short step from hero to mug," a statement many of his successors have amply proved.

6. Disaster in Bilbao 1994

Instead of winning the trophy after the 10-2 aggregate drubbing of Antwerp in the 1994/95 UEFA Cup, Kevin Keegan's team let their defensive frailties get the better of them and lost in the second round to Athletic Bilbao on away goals.

7. Newcastle 1 Sunderland 9 1908

5 December 1908 is a date that will live in infamy for Newcastle fans – the day the Mackems won 9-1 at St James' Park. Bizarrely, the game was poised at 1-1 at half-time, but Sunderland scored six goals in ten minutes to shatter their opponents.

8. Losing to Partizan on penalties 2002

Having done the hard bit – winning 1-0 away thanks to Nobby – United lost by the same score at home and blew the penalty shoot-out to miss out on a place alongside Real Madrid in the Champions League and £12m in the kitty.

9. **Exeter City 4 Newcastle 0** 1981
As FA Cup fifth round exits go, this has to be one of the worst. The Grecians held Newcastle to a draw away and then, in front of the *Sportsnight* TV cameras, went 3-0 up by half-time. They then took pity on United and only scored one more.

10. **"Radford again, oh what a goal"** 1972
Bloody John Motson. If you're going to be the victim of a giant killing, you might as well be involved in the biggest ever. Call this United's contribution to "the romance of the FA Cup" Motty is always talking about. Ronnie Radford didn't crow, recalling: "I was in the right place at the right time. I went home, got some fish and chips, and watched it on telly with the wife. I was back at work on Monday, putting a roof on a house." Oddly, losing 4-1 to Wrexham in the FA Cup in 1978 hurt almost as much.

11. **Upsy Daisy**
After beating the mighty Inter 3-1 over two legs in the 1970/71 Fairs Cup, it was daft to lose in the second round to unknown Hungarian side Pecsi Dozsa, in a penalty shoot-out . With scores tied in the second leg away from home, Newcastle missed their first three penalties. Pecsi Dozsa scored all three of theirs, prompting their fans to invade the pitch. Rules then stipulated that all five penalties had to be taken by both sides. Newcastle scored twice, pointlessly, and bowed out blaming the rutted pitch, a bumpy flight and the host of chances they'd missed in the first leg.

HARTLEPOOL REST HOME
If Newcastle players aren't careful, the Victoria Ground beckons

Joe Allon Newcastle United 1984-87, Hartlepool United 1988-91, 1995-96
Micky Barker Newcastle United 1972-79, Hartlepool United 1982
Viv Busby Newcastle United 1971-72, Hartlepool United manager 1993

John Craggs Newcastle United 1964-71, 1982-83; Hartlepool United 1988 (as assistant coach), November 1989 (as caretaker manager)

Bobby Cummings Newcastle United 1954-56, 1963-65, Hartlepool United 1968-69

David Davidson Newcastle United 1930-37; joined Hartlepool United in June 1937 for £50, left in October.

Eddie Edgar Newcastle United 1973-76; Hartlepool United 1976-79

Tommy Gibb Newcastle United 1968-75; Hartlepool United 1977-79

Steve Howey Newcastle United 1986-2000; Hartlepool United 2005-

Alan Kennedy Newcastle United 1971-78; Hartlepool United November 1987

George Lackenby Newcastle United 1950-56; Hartlepool United 1960-63

HAS ANYONE SEEN BRYAN FERRY?

Famous members of the Toon Army

1. Brian Johnson

The AC/DC shouter/singer tried to buy his way onto the board in 1984 but was rebuffed. He flew in from Florida in February 2000 to see the Toon beat Manchester United 3-0 and told *New Musical Express*: "It was magic. When Big Dunc scored, I exploded oot my seat and so did Keegan" – King Kev was sitting next to him.

2. Tony Blair

No matter how deep or shallow his devotion to Newcastle is, at least, in footballing parlance, he can't be accused of being a glory hunter.

3. Ant & Dec

The irrepressible Geordie pranksters were seen waving to the cameras and looking, well, irrepressible in the 2004/05 FA Cup semi-final tonking by Manchester United. They both list their hobbies as following Newcastle United – the semi-final was an excuse to skip the Baftas – while Ant has been known to sleep in his Newcastle shirt.

4. Robson Green

Geordie actor, a fan since he saw Malcolm Macdonald upfront in 1973/74.

5. Jimmy Nail

His dad played for Huddersfield Town but Nail is a regular at St James' Park.

6. Cardinal Basil Hume

"I lived within the sound of the roar of St James' Park and by the age of nine I went to watch with my father. If the first team wasn't playing I watched the reserves." The Cardinal idolised Wor Jackie but waited 30 years to ask for his autograph – finally getting the valued signature when the two were made Freemen of Newcastle.

7. Kevin Whateley
Geordie actor, played wimpish Newcastle fan Nev in *Auf Wiedersehen, Pet*.

8. Sting
Wrote a Toon FA Cup final song, but as a kid was teased for being a Mackem. His *Black And White Army (Bringing The Pride Back Home)* is a half-decent FA Cup single and less excruciating than his famous insight that Russians love their children too.

9. Honor Blackman
The Londoner who played Pussy Galore is mysteriously listed on the Famous Football Supporters page as a Newcastle United fan. More often seen at Fulham.

10. John McCririck
Malcolm Glazer lookalike, tipster, the United fan other team's fans love to hate.

11. Bryan Ferry
Officially a Newcastle fan, though sightings of the lad from Washington at St James' Park are rare. He did play in goal for Glebe Junior School. For proof, see *http://www.geocities.com/pictorialwashingtonuk/BryanFerry.html*.

HEY BIG SPENDERS!
The 11 most expensive players Newcastle have ever bought

1. **Alan Shearer** £15m 1996
2. **Laurent Robert** £9.5m 2001
3. **Jonathan Woodgate** £9m 2003
4. **Hugo Viana** £8.5m 2002
5. **Duncan Ferguson** £8m 1998
   Jean-Alain Boumsong £8m 2005
7. **Tino Asprilla** £7.5m 1996
8. **Carl Cort** £7m 2000
9. **Les Ferdinand** £6m 1995
   Kieron Dyer £6m 1999
11. **Elena Marcelino** £5.8m 1999

HINESTROZA AND OTHER GREAT MIDDLE NAMES

The name game with Asprilla and 10 other Magpies

Finlay **Ballantyne** Speedie.
Frank **Calvert** Houghton
Bill **Gladstone** Mellor
Faustino Hernan **Hinestroza** Asprilla
Joseph **Kevin** Keegan
Fransiscus **Leonardus** Albertus Koenen
Colin Campbell **McKechnie** Veitch
Alexander **Parrott** Ramsay
Christopher **Roland** Waddle
William **Salmond** Thomson Penman
Neil **Shaka** Hislop

READ THE NEWS TODAY, OH BOY

Newcastle headlines that tell the story

1. "Dyer-bow-lical!"
The Sun hails the sparring session between Kieron Dyer and Lee Bowyer.

2. "Frog on the Tyne"
The *Daily Star* greets Newcastle's signing of Ginola.

3. "United supporter to be next Pope"
The *Newcastle Chronicle* gets over-excited about the 1981 papal election.

4. "God on the Tyne"
FHM's take on Kevin Keegan in 1993.

5. "£13,000 Shackleton Leads Way In 13 Goals United Revel"
Shack's debut in 1946, in a 13-0 win over Newport County, entrances the local press.

6. "Hughie of the magic feet is dead"
The *Newcastle Journal* bemoans Gallacher's suicide.

7. "Resign"
The *Newcastle Chronicle* tells Douglas Hall and Freddy Shepherd to quit after the Spanish brothel affair. They did just that in March 1998 but have since returned.

8. "Plonkers"
The tabloids catch Barry Venison, Steve Howey and Alex Mathie in a Bournemouth wine bar in February 1994 when they ought to have been ten-pin bowling with team-mates. The furore seems quaint now but Venison lost the captaincy over it.

9. "Celebtitty wrestling"
The Sun hails an outbreak of girl-on-girl wrestling as models fight to retain the affections of Peter Crouch and Newcastle new boy Celestine Babayaro.

10. "The Spencer Tracy of football"
Corriere Dello Sport appreciates Sir Bobby Robson's qualities.

11. "Final travesty"
The old *Evening Mail* reacts to Newcastle's 0-0 draw against Bradford City in 1911 – it could easily have been rerun after 1974, 1976, 1998…

IF IT'S TUESDAY, IT MUST BE…

Teams we've played in exotic friendlies – Newcastle's score is listed first

1. Bohemia 3-2 17 May 1905
In this end of season tour, United visited Austria, Prague, then part of the Austro-Hungarian Empire, and Berlin where they beat a Berlin Brits XI 10-1.

2. Cognac 2-1 9 May 1979
Local off-licences being out of stock of the after-dinner tipple, United went straight to the source and beat the locals.

3. Fiji FA 2-0 28 May 1985
Gazza and John Anderson clinched this friendly in the Pacific; just as well as United had lost the first game 3-0.

4. Hajduk Split 2-3 22 May 1960
One from the old days, when friendlies could be a test, not a mismatch or a stroll.

5. Jersey Select XI 6-0 24 July 1975
They define 'select' differently in Jersey.

6. Jim Smith XI 3-6 8 May 1978
Surely the last time Jim organised a team which scored six goals.

7. PFL All-Stars 1-0 18 May 2000
The players, officials and coaches outnumbered the crowd – but still, a vital fixture in the club's grand marketing scheme to sell Steve Howey duvet covers to the almost untapped Trinidadian football merchandising market.

8. Real Madrid 6-1 31 August 1925
Newcastle would thrash Raith Rovers in October by the same score.

9. Santos 2-4 4 June 1972
Like wandering giants, Newcastle and Santos met in Hong Kong. United looked safe at 2-1 with 15 minutes to go till Pelé stepped up a gear. The best goal was by Tony Green – a cracking 35-yard drive that gave the keeper no chance.

10. Sliema Wanderers 4-0 30 May 1977
Newcastle make the Maltese cross.

11. Whitby Town 5-1 13 August 1988
Times being hard, the usual pre-season junket was curtailed and the town where Bram Stoker wrote *Dracula* sent out a team of the living dead.

"THE SPENCER TRACY OF FOOTBALL" WAS ONE DESCRIPTION OF SIR BOBBY ROBSON'S QUALITIES

LIT CRIT

The players autobiographies: The titles say it all

1. **Proud To Be A Geordie** Peter Beardsley
2. **Man On The Run** Mick Channon
3. **Andy Cole** Andy Cole
4. **From St Tropez To St James** David Ginola
5. **Football Inside Out** Alan Gowling
6. **Come In Number 37** Rob Lee
7. **Supermac** Malcolm Macdonald
8. **Never Afraid To Miss** Malcolm Macdonald
9. **My Story So Far** Alan Shearer
10. **My Story** Gazza
11. **Sure It's A Grand Old Team To Play For** Ronnie Simpson

LOCAL HEROES

Cut them and they'd probably bleed black and white

1. Jackie Milburn 1943-1957
Had his ashes scattered over the Gallowgate End.

2. Alan Shearer 1996-
Thousands queued at the Leazes End just to watch him sign for the club.

3. Stan Seymour 1920-1929, 1938-1978 as a director
As a winger who linked so stylishly with McDonald and Gallacher, Seymour was idolised. As a manager/director, judged on silverware, he is the most successful boss since Frank Watt. But his treatment of players left a lot to be desired even by the penny-pinching, autocratic standards of English football administration of his day.

4. Jack Carr 1897-1912
In an era when the team was dominated by Scots, Jack was a local hero. A powerful left-back, he won three titles and spent all his 13 seasons in the game at the club.

5. Peter Beardsley 1982-1987, 1993-1997
Pedro, Modo, Beardo… whatever you call him, Beardsley is a local legend. It's just a pity that, born in Longbenton, he had to make it in Vancouver.

6. Sir John Hall 1990- as chairman and later shareholder
Sir John transformed Newcastle United and, almost as importantly, St James' Park, bringing in Keegan as manager. Depressing as 2004/05 was, United are a long way from where they were when Hall took over. In 1994, he said: "my ambition is to see this club within five years establish itself as one of the top three in the United Kingdom." It's not entirely his fault that he hasn't quite fulfilled that ambition.

7. Colin Veitch 1899-1914
Newcastle Schools' first captain – in 1895 – Veitch was a suave, visionary midfield general. He was almost as influential off the pitch – he was offered the headmaster's job at a local school and asked to stand as a Labour parliamentary candidate. Poet, composer, conductor, actor, musician, Veitch was later banned from the club press box for his stinging, justified criticism of the dreadful Newcastle team of the 1930s.

8. Bobby Robson 1999-2004 as manager
Fans never had any doubt that Robson, a fan since he was a boy in County Durham, felt defeat, victory and humiliation as intensely as anyone on the Gallowgate.

9. Jackie Rutherford 1902-1913
The original Newcastle Flier, Jackie worked in the Tyne shipyards as an apprentice plater. A match-winning winger, he was snapped up for £75 a week, scored 92 goals for Newcastle and left in a dispute over benefit payments. He joined Arsenal later, running down the wing for them when he was 40.

10. Billy Cairns 1933-1944
This Tynesider was a gutsy, no-nonsense, good in the air, shoot on sight striker, who once bagged five goals in a game – against Halifax Town in the wartime season 1939/40. His father and grandfather were famous runners on Tyneside.

11. Paul Gascoigne 1980-1988
The Mars bars which greeted Gazza on his return to St James' Park were angry proof of the hopes invested in him on Tyneside.

LOWEST OF THE LOW

11 seasons to erase from your memory banks

1. 1933/34

Having come fifth in Division One in 1932/33, nobody envisaged the dire campaign that awaited Andy Cunningham's men. The sole high point was a Christmas goalfest with a 7-3 victory over Everton and a 9-2 demolition of Liverpool. One win in the last 14 games condemned the Magpies to the drop after 36 years in the top flight.

2. 1957/58

Ten home defeats set a club record that heralded the end of the Directors' Committee's handling of team affairs. United avoided relegation on goal difference, thanks to 22-goal saviour Len White.

3. 1960/61

Hard to believe a team with Len White and Ivor Allchurch upfront could be relegated. But, with a defence that conceded 109 times, not even the 86 goals of an attack that included George Eastham could avoid relegation to the old Division Two.

4. 1966/67

Low points included two 3-0 defeats at the hands of Sunderland and a 6-0 defeat to a Blackpool side who only amassed 21 points all season. Newcastle came third bottom, the lowest league placing of Joe Harvey's 13 years at St James' Park.

5. 1977/78

A record run of ten straight defeats left Newcastle rock bottom of the table by mid-October. French side Bastia inspired by Johnny Rep ended Newcastle's UEFA Cup campaign in the second round. Manager Richard Dinnis was replaced by disciplinarian Bill McGarry. "Player Power" founders such as Tommy Craig and Alan Kennedy were sold under McGarry's regime but the hardline didn't save Newcastle from relegation. The Magpies finished second bottom, conceding 78 league goals.

6. 1980/81

At the start of the campaign United needed just 35 goals to reach the 5000th league goal milestone. That this feat was not achieved until 1981/82 tells its own story. Arthur Cox replaced Bill McGarry in early September but to little effect.

7. 1986/87

A nine game unbeaten run starting in early March secured the First Division status of Willie McFaul's side. Goals from Paul Goddard, bought from West Ham for a club record fee, arrested a slide that threatened relegation. Peter Beardsley had seen enough by July and was sold to Liverpool for a national record of £1.9m.

8. 1988/89

Not even £2.6m from the sale of Paul Gascoigne could save Newcastle from relegation. Of McFaul's four signings only John Hendrie, with five goals, made much impact. McFaul had gone by October with Jim Smith taking over. With a record low of just three home league wins, Newcastle were relegated to Division Two.

9. 1991/92

A season to forget but one that featured one of the club's most memorable moments. Steve Walsh's 90th-minute own goal on the last day of the season ensured Newcastle's safety, a gripping finale to a dismal campaign. Up until Kevin Keegan's arrival in February, Ossie Ardiles's youthful side had seemed destined for Division Three. Defensive shortcomings didn't help – 84 league goals were shipped.

10. 1998/99

Andreas Andersson, Silvio Maric, Ruud Gullit, unsexy football, second successive bout of FA Cup final heartache. Enough already.

11. 2004/05

The misery is too fresh in the memory for you to need reminding.

MACKEM MOMENTS

Great Tyne triumphs over Wear

1. "Remember 9-1"

Boxing Day 1955, at Roker Park, and Sunderland are 6-1 down. But Milburn isn't giving up – he shouts at team-mates "Remember 9-1!" – the scoreline by which the Wearsiders had beaten Newcastle in 1908. Sadly, an injury to winger Bobby Mitchell with 25 minutes to go means Milburn can't extract full revenge. Newcastle console themselves by winning their home game, the next day, against Sunderland 4-2.

JACKIE MILBURN'S TESTIMONIAL XI ON 10 MAY 1967

Gordon Marshall

Cecil Irwin   Frank Clark   George Kinnell

Dave Elliott   Jim Iley   George Herd

Wyn Davies   Neil Martin

Jackie Milburn   Bryan 'Pop' Robson

Jackie Milburn's testimonial XI on 10 May 1967, ten years after his retirement, attracted a crowd of 46,000. "I was worried no one would turn up" said Wor Jackie

2. Season's greetings

Seasons don't end much better than this. In 1996/97, Newcastle United clinched a Champions League slot, while Sunderland and Middlesbrough slid back down to what was then Division One. On the final day of the season, both teams could have stayed up if they'd won – but Sunderland lost 1-0 to Coventry City and Boro drew 1-1 at Leeds United. Newcastle, meanwhile, won 5-0 at home to Nottingham Forest.

3. A merry Christmas

There are few better ways to mark 25 December than hammering Sunderland away from home. In 1951, a Newcastle side powered by Milburn, Robledo and Mitchell beats the Wearsiders 4-1 at Roker Park. The glossy book *Today's The Day* sums this up nicely with the headline: "Sunderland hammered in Christmas panto".

4. So you want to be a record breaker?

You don't have to be the best – you can, as Sunderland proved in 2002/03, be the worst and achieve record-breaking statistical significance. Sunderland ended the season with the lowest-ever points tally – 19 – in Premiership history. Other Premiership records set this season by a Sunderland team managed by Peter Reid, Howard Wilkinson and Mick McCarthy included the lowest goals total, the lowest number of wins and the longest losing streak. The end of season report by the BBC included the magical line: "Lows: the period encompassing August until May".

5. Sunderland 1 Charlton Athletic 3

On 1 February 2003, Sunderland lose at home to Charlton. Nothing too unusual in that, but the Mackems excel themselves by scoring all three goals for their opponents. The first Charlton goal is deflected by Sunderland's Stephen Wright into the net. Cometh the hour, cometh the man, and up steps Michael Proctor, to deflect a Thomas Sorensen save into his own net and then find the killer touch from a Charlton corner to give the south Londoners a 3-0 lead and set another record – for scoring the most own goals in a Premiership match. Pity this isn't on video.

6. Alex Tait's hat-trick

For such a skilful centre-forward, Tait didn't score too many goals – ten in 34 games – but, moving out to the right wing, he grabbed a memorable hat-trick against Sunderland on 22 December 1956 which cemented his status as a crowd favourite. United had the hex over the Mackems in the 1950s and, with Tait's help, won 6-2.

7. The "sad Mackem bastards" T-shirt

Famously worn by Lee Clark, after he'd joined Sunderland from Newcastle.

8. Hughie Gallacher's day

Sunderland were feeling cocky after they had thrashed us 5-2 earlier in the 1928/29 season, but Gallacher scored twice and, with the aid of an own goal, United won 4-3.

9. "I wish we had supporters like Newcastle's…"

In 1982, Mackems chairman Tom Cowle admits that, if they'd signed Keegan, fans would not have queued up for tickets. His successor Bob Murray later whined: "we're stuck between a massive city that's vibrant like Newcastle – and Middlesbrough."

10. 6-1 St James' Park, 1920/21

Any time you put six past Sunderland is worth commemorating. Neil Harris, Stan Seymour and Andy Smailes were the stars on this great October afternoon in 1920.

11. "Good evening Newcastle!"

David Bowie's cheery greeting to the Roker Park crowd on his 1987 Glass Spider tour.

> YOU DON'T HAVE TO BE THE BEST TO BE A RECORD BREAKER, AS SUNDERLAND PROVED IN 2002/03

MOST CAPPED PLAYER TO PLAY FOR NEWCASTLE

Not all of these caps were earned while at United...

1. **Kenny Sansom** England 86 caps
2. **Gary Speed** Wales 85 caps
3. **John Barnes** England 79 caps
   Patrick Kluivert Holland 79 caps
5. **Stuart Pearce** England 78 caps
6. **Ian Rush** Wales 73 caps
7. **Shay Given** Ireland 68 caps
   Ivor Allchurch Wales 68 caps
9. **David McCreery** Northern Ireland 67 caps
10. **Alan Shearer** England 63 caps
    Kevin Keegan England 63 caps
    Marc Hottiger Switzerland 63 caps

MOST PROLIFIC GOALSCORERS IN A SEASON SINCE THE WAR

The figures for these net busters are for league goals only

1. **Andy Cole** 34 goals 1993/94
2. **George Robledo** 33 goals 1951/52
3. **Micky Quinn** 32 goals 1989/90
4. **Charlie Wayman** 30 goals 1946/47
5. **Len White** 28 goals 1959/60
   Len White 28 goals 1960/61
7. **Kevin Keegan** 27 goals 1983/84
8. **Len White** 25 goals 1958/59
   Les Ferdinand 25 goals 1995/96
   Alan Shearer 25 goals 1996/97
11. **David Kelly** 24 goals 1992/93

N

NAMESAKES

Architects, comics, folk musicians... a talented lot these United doppelgangers

Frank Clark An English landscape architect and garden historian.
Paul Dalglish As senior vice president, business integration, Paul has overall responsibility for integrating new clients into Accenture Business Services.
Wyn Davies Has been collecting telegraph keys for many years.
Duncan Ferguson Writer and performer of traditional Scottish music and folk rock.
Joe Harvey He reproduces charming Newfoundland outport furniture in pine, with natural finishes and hand-rubbed antique oil.
Robert Lee Professor, PhD 1990, University of Arizona. Areas of interest: numerical techniques, finite element/finite difference methods, hybrid methods.
Malcolm Macdonald Distinguished writer on classical music. Author of *Varese: Astronomer In Sound*.
Bobby Mitchell Winner of the Las Vegas Comedy Festival, 2002.
Mick Quinn Author of *Four Steps Of Awakened Living*, sample quote from blurb:"In a moment of despair he asked a question of the universe. In that same moment a bottle washed up at his feet. The message inside is the core of this book."
Bryan Robson Performs football miracles in the Midlands.
Len White Special effects, *Spider Man 2*.

NEARLY MEN

11 who could have played for United

1. Roberto Baggio A £9m deal wrecked by Il Divino Ponytail's £64,000-a-week wage demands – in 1995.
2. Jesper Blomqvist Even Keegan could only have so many wingers at once.
3. Alen Boksic Could have signed instead of Asprilla but Newcastle opted for Tino.
4. Mel Charles The board couldn't make their mind up so the opportunity passed.
5. Brad Friedel Couldn't get a work permit.

6. Alan Hansen Gordon Lee allegedly didn't like Scottish players.
7. Denis Law Didn't fancy Newcastle.
8. Francis Lee See above.
9. Ray Wilson Too settled in Huddersfield.
10. Jackie Milburn Almost re-signed after leaving Linfield in 1959. Director Stan Seymour declared Jackie could do well in the local minor leagues and vetoed the deal. Not a nice thing to say, but Seymour was probably right.
11. Wayne Rooney Give Freddy his due, this was always just a wheeze for making Manchester United write out a much larger cheque.

OLD KING COAL

Newcastle stars with connections to mining

Harry Clifton First played for Lintz Colliery in 1932.
Ron Batty Joined Newcastle from East Tanfield Colliery in 1945.
Bobby Cowell Worked down a pit.
William Gallantree First impressed for Harton Colliery in 1930.
Ron Greener First starred for Easington Colliery in 1950.
Kevin Keegan The son of a miner from Hetton-Le-Hole.
Jackie Milburn Worked as a fitter at Hazelrigg Colliery – until he needed every Saturday off to play for Newcastle.
Len Shackleton Briefly worked as a labourer at Hazelrigg Colliery – but was terrified by his first experience of going down to the coalface in the miner's cage.
Alan Shoulder Worked down a pit.
Stan Seymour A joiner in a local pit.
Charlie Wayman A miner from Bishop Auckland.
And **Bobby Robson** was, famously, the son of a Durham coal miner.

ONE HIT WONDERS

For this lot. once was enough. There are 78 players who have racked up just one first-team appearance but we're only listing a randomly chosen 11.

1. **Justin Fashanu** 29/10/1991
2. **Steve Guppy** 26/10/1994
3. **George Mole** 31/3/1900
4. **Archie Mowatt** 17/12/1898
5. **Rob McKinnon** 7/9/1985
6. **James Coppinger** 26/8/2000
7. **Eddie Edgar** 6/3/1976
8. **Keen Errington** 18/10/1930
9. **John Hope** 5/5/1969
10. **Neville Black** 24/9/1952
11. **Haynes** 9/3/1895

Haynes, a local lad who played once as left-back, doesn't have a full name – indeed some believe he is really United keeper John Hynd, a full-back in his younger days.

ONES THAT GOT AWAY

Players we should have signed or kept

1. Alan Shearer

Newcastle had a look at one of the most promising schoolboys on their doorstep and gave Alan Shearer a trial in goal.

2. Frank Clark

The left-back gave Newcastle absolutely magnificent service. Then United decided to throw him on the soccer scrapheap by giving the local boy a free transfer, so Clarkie joined Nottingham Forest and won the European Cup.

3. Jon Dahl Tomasson

There's no doubt that Newcastle did not make the most of Danish striker Jon Dahl Tomasson when Kenny Dalglish signed him from Dutch club Heerenveen for £3.9m in 1997. Dalglish failed to play him in his preferred position as a striker through the middle. It came as no surprise when, after a disappointing season, he was on his way back to Holland and Feyenoord for a knock-down price. Newcastle then had to watch as the Dane turned into a lethal striker with Feyenoord and AC Milan. The Newcastle reject was second-highest scorer in the 2002 World Cup finals.

4. Paul Gascoigne

Newcastle knew Gazza was special. But United weren't special enough for him. He left in 1988 after four years in the black and white shirt to become one of the most talked about players in the world, mainly with Spurs, Rangers and Lazio, winning 57 England caps. After losing three local boys – Peter Beardsley, Chris Waddle and Gazza – the board decided United would no longer be a selling club.

5. Sylvain Distin

Newcastle fans loved French defender Sylvain Distin when he was on loan from Paris Saint-Germain in 2001/02. A permanent deal seemed a formality. But after agreeing a £3.8m fee with PSG, Newcastle could not settle personal terms with Distin. So off he went to Manchester City where Kevin Keegan made him captain. Graeme Souness tried – and failed – to buy Distin for £6m in January 2005.

6. Alan Thompson

Geordie boy Alan Thompson thought he had fulfilled his dream when he joined his beloved Newcastle United, but it became a nightmare when he only managed 16 appearances in three years. It broke his heart when Kevin Keegan let him go to Bolton Wanderers for £2.5m in July 1993. At Bolton, the left-sided midfielder married a local lass and won two promotions to the Premiership in 1995 and 1997. Tomma was so established that Aston Villa paid £7.2m for him and he then joined Celtic where he became a big favourite. All he ever wanted to do was play for Newcastle.

7. Peter Schmeichel

Newcastle sent a United scout to Copenhagen to watch young Danish keeper Peter Schmeichel play for Brondby. And back he came with the verdict "Not good enough". While Newcastle dithered, Manchester United pounced.

8. Sami Hyypia

When Hyypia was playing for MyPa 47 in his native Finland, he was invited to train with Newcastle so then manager Kevin Keegan could look at him. It was all happening at Newcastle then and amidst all the activity Hyypia was allowed to slip back to Finland. But he soon became a captain and cult hero at Anfield.

9. Alan Kennedy

When Newcastle sold Alan Kennedy to Liverpool for £300,000 in 1978 the money was welcome. But not as welcome as Kennedy was made at Liverpool. The man dubbed Barney Rubble won an amazing 14 winners medals with Liverpool. With Newcastle, all he won was a loser's medal after that 1974 FA Cup final defeat. He is the only British player to score the winning goal in two European Cup finals.

10. Peter Beardsley

Was starring for the renowned Wallsend Boys Club when Newcastle sent their scout and former player Geoff Allen to watch the Geordie boy go through his full repertoire of tricks. But United were beaten to the punch by another manager, their former war horse and one of their greatest skippers Bobby Moncur, then managing Carlisle. Moncs even let Beardsley live in his own home for six months. It cost United £110,000 to get Beardsley back years later from Vancouver Whitecaps.

11. Steve Bruce

Another former Wallsend Boys Club player who waited for the call from Newcastle United. He waited. And he waited. In the end he got sick of waiting and headed for Gillingham. And while at Gillingham, Newcastle actually watched him but decided against signing probably the greatest centre-half never to play for England. He did get the chance to manage Newcastle after Sir Bobby Robson was sacked in August 2004. But he had just signed a five-year contract with Birmingham City.

ORDNANCE SURVEY XI

A team whose names you might find on an Ordnance Survey map...

Michael Bridges 2004-
John Cape 1930-1934
Phil Cave, youth player
Jimmy Fell 1962-1963
David Ford 1969-1971
Tony Green 1971-1973
Jimmy Hill (not that one) 1957-1958
Kris Gate, youth player
Oswald Park 1924-1931
Glenn Roeder 1983-1989
Ed Wood 1928-1930

PIG FARMING, PIANO PLAYING AND SELLING ADVERTISING

Jobs Newcastle players have taken to make ends meet. Note: Chris Waddle's sausage-making is mentioned so often we've chosen to ignore it in this 11.

1. Advertising manager for Golf Monthly
John Connolly, brilliantly inconsistent on the wing for Bill McGarry's Newcastle from 1978-1980, worked as advertising manager for *Golf Monthly* magazine.

2. Art dealer
Benny Arentoft won the 1969 Fairs Cup and later, in his home city of Copenhagen, he was an art dealer, journalist and council employee.

3. Butcher of Gateshead
Bill Imrie, a gutsy, capable right-half and skipper, couldn't save a poor Newcastle side from the drop in 1933/34, and ran a butcher's shop in Gateshead.

4. Consultant to Major League Soccer
David McCreery played in the 1982 World Cup for Northern Ireland. After leaving football, he was a paid adviser to the Major League Soccer organisation.

5. Delivering beer
Michael James Mahoney was a safe pair of hands for Newcastle in the 1970s and brought the same consistency to his job as a beer delivery driver in Los Angeles.

6. Glazing
Bobby Shinton had trained as a glazer. His stay at Newcastle United was not an especially happy one and, retiring from the game in 1985, he went back to glazing.

7. Insurance man
Bobby Moncur was a versatile devil – a superb central defender, a fine golfer and an

accomplished sailor who opened his own yachting company. Working for an insurance company is one of the duller jobs on his packed CV.

8. Opening a snooker centre
Patrick Howard was such a no-nonsense centre-half for Newcastle in the 1970s, it is no surprise he became the imperious owner of a snooker centre in Bury.

9. Pig farmer
Mirandinha had worked down a salt mine as a kid and, when football couldn't pay his way, he branched out into pig farming in Sao Paolo.

10. Playing a pink piano in a rock band
Even for a winger, Trevor Hockey was, well, different, once owning a velvet-covered car, so his stint playing a pink piano in a rock band seemed entirely in character.

11. Postman in Gravesend
Arthur Horsfield, whose career at Newcastle lasted eight games and three goals in 1969, later became a man of letters – like Kevin Hecto and Peter Bonetti – as reliable on his postal round as he was on the pitch for Newcastle, Swindon and Charlton.

POINTLESS SEASONS

Lowest point tallies – for seasons with 34 league games or more

1. 1977/78 21st Division One 22 points
2. 1898/99 13th Division One 30 points
3. 1988/89 20th Division One 31 points
4. 1960/61 21st Division One 32 points
   1957/58 19th Division One 32 points
   1914/15 15th Division One 32 points
   1902/03 14th Division One 32 points
8. 1966/67 20th Division One 33 points
9. 1933/34 21st Division One 34 points
   1912/13 14th Division One 34 points
11. 1930/31 17th Division One 36 points
   1937/38 19th Division Two 36 points
   1956/57 17th Division One 36 points

PRINCES OF WALES

Welsh wizards to have worn the zebra shirt – the degree of wizardry does vary

1. **Ivor Allchurch** inside-forward, 1958-62
2. **Craig Bellamy** striker, 2001-
3. **Paul Bodin** left-back, 1991-92
4. **Ollie Burton** centre-half, 1963-73
5. **Ellis Davies** inside-forward, 1951-58
6. **Wyn Davies** centre-forward, 1966-71
7. **Tom Evans** left-back, 1927-29
8. **Dave Hollins** goalkeeper, 1961-67
9. **William Hughes** right-back, 1908-10
10. **Ian Rush** striker, 1997-98
11. **Ron Williams** centre-forward, 1933-35

THE PRIZE GUYS

11 United award winners

1. **Craig Bellamy** PFA Young Player of the Year, 2002
2. **Andy Cole** Runner-up for European Golden Boot in 1993/94 – to David Taylor of Porthmadog. Cole was top scorer in Premiership in the same season with 34 goals and PFA Young Player of the Year, 1994
3. **Paul Gascoigne** PFA Young Player of the Year, 1988
4. **Jermaine Jenas** PFA Young Player of the Year, 2003
5. **Malcolm Macdonald** Top scorer in Division One, 1974/75, 21 goals
6. **George Robledo** Top scorer in Division One, 1951/52, 33 goals
7. **Sir Bobby Robson** More than deserved his knighthood in June 2002
8. **Micky Quinn** Top scorer in Division Two, 1989/90, 32 goals
9. **Alan Shearer** Third in ballot for the Ballon D'Or, 1996; top scorer in Premiership, 1996/97, 25 goals; PFA Player of the Year, 1996/97
10. **Albert Shepherd** Top scorer in Football League, 1910/11, with 25 goals
11. **Charlie Wayman** Top scorer in Division Two, 1946/47, 32 goals

PROGRAMMES! PROGRAMMES!

No one's ever got rich trading Newcastle programmes

1. Newcastle v Barnsley 4 September 1935 £1,000
The attendance at this Division Two game was 21,000. But not many of them could have kept their programme as this is now worth a four-figure sum. Pre-war Newcastle programmes are extremely rare – and hence very valuable.

2. Chelsea v Newcastle 1931/32 FA Cup semi-final £1,000
Newcastle, pitted against Hughie Gallacher's Chelsea, prevailed 2-1 at Leeds Road, Huddersfield and would go on to win the final.

3. Newcastle v Blackpool 1951 FA Cup final programme £70-100
The revelations inside include: "Newcastle used to pay their players a shilling a goal".

4. Newcastle v Arsenal 1952 FA Cup final programme £60
The second of the Magpies' three FA Cup wins.

5. Newcastle v Chelsea April 1956 £35
Newcastle programmes from the 1950s aren't quite as rare but still valuable, as this Division One souvenir shows.

6. Newcastle v Manchester City 1955 FA Cup final £30-40
The last time Newcastle won some proper silverware in England. The programme for the semi-final, against York, is rare, and could fetch £25 and over.

7. Newcastle v Ujpesti Dozsa Fairs Cup final 1969 home programme £10-40

8. Anderlecht v Newcastle Fairs Cup quarter-final 1970 £8
Newcastle did a decent job defending their trophy, only losing to that season's finalists Anderlecht in the last eight on away goals.

9. Ferencvaros v Newcastle UEFA Cup 1996 £7
Reasonably rare souvenir of one of the great Newcastle Eurovisions.

10. Newcastle v Inter Milan Inter-Cities Fairs Cup 1970 £5
Ridiculously cheap souvenir of a night when United humbled the mighty Inter.

11. Newcastle v Hereford United FA Cup 1972 £4
The programme notes presciently point out Hereford "haven't come here to lose

and they also know that giant-killing acts have happened before and will no doubt happen again." With a psychic editor and a striking cover, this is a classic edition.

PUNDITS

Magpies who have opined on TV, radio or in newsprint

John Barnes Less interesting for his punditry than his dress sense, now hosting his own football night on Channel 5.
Kevin Gallacher Radio Rovers, Blackburn.
Paul Gascoigne One World Cup wonder on ITV.
David Ginola Briefly incomprehensible on BBC1.
Brian Kilcline Match summariser, BBC Radio Leeds.
Malcolm Macdonald On Century Radio.
Jackie Milburn Wrote for the *News Of The World* in more innocent times.
Gavin Peacock On multi-channel subs bench for tournaments like the African Nations Cup.
Len Shackleton Wrote for the *Daily Express* and *Sunday People*.
Alan Shearer Warming up on Sky and BBC1.
Barry Venison Having had his ITV slot usurped by former Smoggie Andy Townsend, now hangs out on Channel 5 with Barnesy.

QUICK OFF THE MARK

Dream debuts don't always mean a player will fulfil their dreams

1. Hughie Gallacher

Fans were thrilled by their new star Scottish striker, until he walked onto the pitch for his debut against Everton in December 1925 and the Gallowgate saw how small he was (5ft 5in). In the silence, the Scotsman recalled: "Never have I been more conscious of my size." But after 30 minutes, he collected the ball with his back to goal, turned, ran between the Everton defenders and scored a classic goal. He scored another and made the third as the Magpies drew 3-3. In his first eight games in a Newcastle shirt, he scored 15 goals, a feat no one has emulated since.

2. Kevin Keegan
The Geordie Messiah's first coming started with a day of astonishing euphoria as, in the first game of 1982/83, against QPR, he scores the only goal of the game.

3. Jackie Milburn (1)
Against Barnsley, on 5 January 1946, in the third round of the FA Cup, Milburn scores twice as the Tykes are thumped 4-2.

4. Jackie Milburn (2)
Against Bury, wearing the No9 shirt for the first time, dreadfully nervous that he's not up to the tradition embodied by the likes of Gallacher and Wayman, he scores a hat-trick on 18 October 1947 against Bury and the Magpies win 5-3.

5. Malcolm Macdonald
On his home debut against Liverpool on 21 August 1971, Supermac scored a hat-trick – one goal a penalty – prompting choruses of "Supermac, superstar, how many goals have you scored so far?"

6. Duncan Neale
It was quite a jump from Ilford in the Isthmian League to the First Division and Newcastle but, on his debut against Fulham on 24 August 1960, the 20-year-old attacking midfielder seemed certain to make it. He scored two memorable goals as the Cottagers were hammered 7-2. Neale's career never got any better than this. He left in 1962 having added just ten goals to the brace scored on his debut.

7. Micky Quinn
The Mighty Quinn song never seemed more apt than on Sumo's debut against Leeds United in August 1999 when he scored four. The Magpies won 5-2. Most remarkable of all, Quinn raced from the halfway line to score his fourth, latching on to a telling through pass and slotting the ball home past Mervyn Day.

8. Bryan Robson
Pop scored on his debut, the game's only goal against Charlton in September 1964, but he'd have to wait for Wyn Davies's arrival in October 1966 to make a real impact.

9. Len Shackleton

A double hat-trick against Newport County on his debut in October 1946. Shack, then the club's record signing at £13,000, shrugged off the burden of the big transfer fee as easily as he shrugged off Newport's defenders. In less than two years, he would be gone to Sunderland, a clown prince in exile.

10. Albert Shepherd

In a dream debut against Nottingham Forest in November 1908, Shepherd grabbed a goal as Newcastle won 4-0 away. On his home debut, in the Wearside derby, he scored a rocket of a penalty. His joy was marred by the fact that, as the final whistle blew, his goal was the one in the scoreline Newcastle 1 Sunderland 9. This didn't, though, deter Shepherd who would score over 90 goals for the Magpies.

11. Liam Tuohy

On 24 August 1960, Fulham must have been in an unusually generous mood. It wasn't just that they shipped seven goals but that six were scored by players who weren't first-team regulars. Tuohy, bought to replace Bobby Mitchell on the wing, had a delightful afternoon, scoring in both halves. But he would score only seven more before leaving St James' Park for Shamrock Rovers.

> "EFFING HELL, ARE WE HAVING A MINUTE'S SILENCE OR WHAT?" DAVID BATTY MOURNS KEEGAN'S EXIT

QUOTE UNQUOTE
Dummies, packs of cards, white socks... all that and more

1. "All you've got to do is score a goal. These foreigners are all the same, they'll collapse like a pack of cards. They've got no gumption"
Joe Harvey's half-time team talk in the second leg of the 1969 Inter-Cities Fairs Cup final against Ujpesti Dozsa. United, 2-0 down after 45 minutes, win 3-2.

2. "As God is my judge, the man was in play. It was a goal"
Referee Percy Harper defends his decision to let Newcastle's controversial equaliser stand against Arsenal in the 1932 FA Cup final.

3. "I've heard of players selling dummies but this club keeps buying them"
Len Shackleton's famous observation about United's transfer dealings has lost little of its relevance today. His other great bon mot about Newcastle in the 1970s was:

"Newcastle have had terrible luck with injuries – the players keep recovering."

4. "The white socks will give us an advantage over the opposition"
Ruud Gullit's hopes for the new kit – with added white socks – are soon dashed.

5. "If you put 11 black and white dogs on the field you'd get 30,000 coming to watch"
Sir Matt Busby said this and there have been times when the board seemed tempted to prove him right.

6. "Not a team-sheet but a suicide note"
Journalist Tim Rich on Gullit's Shearer-less line up for the 1999 Tyne and Wear derby.

7. "F***ing hell, are we having a minute's silence or what?"
David Batty's morale-boosting dressing-room response to Keegan's resignation.

8. "I'm having a Jon Dahl Tomasson today"
What players said if they were having a bad day in training when the Swede was at his most ineffectual in 1997.

9. "If I've got it wrong, there's a bullet with my name on it"
King Kev puts his job on the line after selling Andy Cole in 1995.

10. "If we as a club – or Bill McGarry as an individual – had wanted a black and white army, we would have introduced conscription"
The Newcastle United programme condemns pitch invasions in 1980/81.

11. "Say your prayers, Reds. We Geordies are out for glory and we'll get it too"
Malcolm Macdonald proves he's not psychic, just big-mouthed, as he motivates the Liverpool side in the week before the 1974 FA Cup final. He says he was misquoted.

READ ALL ABOUT IT

Half-decent Newcastle books

1. Geordie Messiah Alan Oliver
Alan helped with this *Rough Guide*, so recommending this feels a bit odd, but this does for Newcastle United in the Keegan era what *All Played Out* did for Italia 90. Reading this is almost like being there.

2. The Magpies A Day In The Life Mike Bolam
Be warned: once you start dipping into this you'll never stop. His *Little Book Of Black And White Quotes* is quite compelling too.

3. The Toon Roger Hutchinson
Sprightly, readable, unbiased but not boring biography of the club.

4. Jackie Milburn A Man Of Two Halves Jack Milburn
Wor Jackie wrote his own book *Golden Goals* but his son's is the more insightful read. Milburn is such a hero it is a shock to read that he had to work in a scrapyard after hanging his boots up. An engaging read from a more Corinthian age.

5. Shirt Of Legends Paul Joannou
The story of Newcastle's great No9s isn't quite as compelling as watching them but it's still a cracking read. The earlier stuff – tales of Shepherd and Gallacher – is especially inspiring. His 100th anniversary tome is another must.

6. My Autobiography Kevin Keegan
A joint production with Bob Harris, this is a good, candid read. The incidental stuff – players who call in sick with migraines on matchday – is more compelling than some of the stuff which made headlines. For some reason this is more gripping than Bob Harris's other Toon-related collaboration: Bobby Robson's memoirs.

7. Geordie Passion Mark Hannen
"When play was on the far side you couldn't see the ball or the players' ankles or feet". A fan's eye-witness view of the Toon from 1969 to 1994. In his first season as a supporter, he outed Alan Foggon as a "right fatso" and struggled to control his bitterness as his dad explained how Newcastle had been booted out of Europe despite scoring the same number of goals as Anderlecht. Such happy times.

8. Toons Of Glory Joe Bernstein
Slender, passionate tome celebrating seven great Newcastle teams, the finest of which – according to a jury of former players with Malcolm Macdonald as the foreman – was the 1951 FA Cup winning team.

9. The United Alphabet Paul Joannou
Out of date but still addictive – and authoritative.

10. Magnificent Obsession Colin Malam
Covers a very similar patch to *Geordie Messiah*, but Malam makes good use of his access to Sir John Hall to round out the picture.

11. The Hughie Gallacher Story Paul Joannou
United's club historian strikes again. Hard to find but worth the effort.

RECORD TRANSFERS FOR STRIKERS

With No9 being a sacred shirt at Newcastle. the club has usually been willing to spend serious money to fill that role with the right player

1. Alan Shearer £15m, Blackburn, July 1996
2. Les Ferdinand £6m, QPR, June 1995
3. Andy Cole £1.75m, Bristol City, March 1993
4. Mirandinha £575,000, Palmeiras, August 1987
5. Paul Goddard £415,000, West Ham United, November 1986
6. Peter Withe £200,000, Nottingham Forest, August 1978
7. Malcolm Macdonald £180,000, Fulham, May 1971
8. Wyn Davies £80,000, Bolton Wanderers, October 1966
9. Barrie Thomas £45,000, Scunthorpe United, January 1962
10. George Lowrie £18,500, Coventry City, March 1948
11. Hughie Gallacher £6,500-7,000, Airdrie, December 1925

SAFE HANDS

Newcastle's goalkeeping tradition isn't as great as that of Arsenal, Leicester City or Chesterfield, but not all United keepers have been dodgy.

1. Shay Given 1997-
Needs no introduction to fans. His performance against Tottenham in the 2004/05 FA Cup summed up what he's brought to the club. He must get more shot-stopping practice than any other keeper in top flight football except, perhaps, Real Madrid's Iker Casillas.

2. Jimmy Lawrence 1904-22
Jimmy took over first-team goalkeeping duties in 1904 and didn't relinquish the jersey until 1922, after 507 appearances. He had, noted an early book *Association Football & The Men Who Made It*, "the approved coolness, insouciance and resource which are the hallmark of the heaven sent keeper". He would have won more than one Scotland cap if not for prejudice against players who had moved to England.

3. Jack Fairbrother 1947-52
A truly great keeper who never got his due from the England selectors when at his peak in the 1940s. A former copper, he wore police gloves in goal occasionally as a joke. But his goalkeeping was unfussy, based on positional sense rather than superb reflexes. He believed if you made too many spectacular saves you couldn't really be a great keeper because your sense of position and angles wasn't good enough.

4. Willie McFaul 1966-75
Fondly remembered for a holy trinity of fine saves – a penalty stop in the 1969 Inter-Cities Fairs Cup semi-final against Rangers, a tip-over in the final against Ujpesti Dozsa and a fine stop against Burnley in the 1974 FA Cup semi-final. He also scored a penalty against Pecsi Dozsa – in the penalty shoot-out in the 1970 Fairs Cup. It was his bad luck to be a gifted Northern Irish keeper at the same time as Pat Jennings.

5. Ronnie Simpson 1951-60

Small for a keeper but with astonishing reflexes, Ronnie Simpson fought back from injury to win the European Cup with Jock Stein's Celtic in 1967. That achievement has tended to overshadow his contribution between the sticks at Newcastle in the 1950s, when he won two FA Cup finals. He was stricken with a serious muscle injury and sold, prematurely as it proved, by Charlie Mitten in 1960.

6. Pavel Srnicek 1990-98

Prone to the odd error, the Czech keeper improved tremendously after arriving on Tyneside in 1991, improving his English and composure on crosses, though his decision-making was never flawless. A former Czech Army soldier, he never shirked his duty and was a magnificent shot stopper. One save against Everton, when he twisted in mid-air, was chosen by Gordon Banks as one of the ten best he ever saw.

7. Albert McInroy 1929-34

A confident, talented, witty keeper who won the FA Cup with Newcastle in 1932. Only a row with the directors over a benefit prevented McInroy from giving them the kind of service he'd given the Wearsiders, where he'd been sound for 227 games.

8. Shaka Hislop 1995-98

A gifted shot stopper, unlucky to be in a four-way battle for the Newcastle No1 spot with Given, Srnicek and, er, Mike Hooper. A thoughtful, brave and useful keeper with the ability, every now and then, to make a truly stupendous save.

9. Gordon Marshall 1963-68

After Simpson left, the club shuffled goalkeepers for a while until Marshall, more consistent than his rivals Dave Hollins and Bryan Harvey, took charge. Not afraid to dive in where feet were flying, he was ever present in 1964/65 when Newcastle clawed their way out of Division Two.

10. Charles Watts 1896-1906

Robust, agile and with a knack for punching a ball over distance, Charles Watts was known to make the odd blooper. But he was the club's first recognised keeper and, in 1897, saved the same penalty kick three times against Burnley.

11. Martin Thomas 1983-88

It's hard for fans who saw Thomas in goal not to wonder what might have been if he hadn't suffered so many injuries. First-choice keeper after Newcastle returned to Division One in 1985, he joined the club on loan, trying to get some first team experience after losing his place at Bristol Rovers due to a badly dislocated finger.

SCORING FOR FUN

Stupid expression really – but here are 11 seasons when United were most prolific

1. 1951/52 98 goals
2. 1926/27 96 goals
3. 1946/47 95 goals
4. 1934/35 89 goals
   1954/55 89 goals
6. 1935/36 88 goals
7. 1960/61 86 goals
8. 1955/56 85 goals
9. 1925/26 84 goals
10. 1959/60 82 goals
11. 1966/67 81 goals
Figures refer to league goals only.

SEVENTH WONDER

No9 is the prime number but No7 is not without significance for United

1. 7 January 1950 The day Supermac was born.
2. Seven is also the number of bells Alan Shearer has not promised to knock out of former strike partner Craig Bellamy.
3. In **seven years** from 1905 to 1911, Newcastle United reached five FA Cup finals, winning the trophy just once.
4. Newcastle have never yet put **seven goals** past Sunderland in a Tyne and Wear derby, but they have beaten them 6-1 and 6-2.
5. Lee Bowyer was banned for **seven games** after fighting with Kieron Dyer against Aston Villa.
6. Newcastle have inflicted Manchester United's record home defeat – beating the Red Devils **7-1** at Old Trafford in September 1927.
7. Newcastle have also put **seven** goals past Manchester United in two other games: a **7-4** thriller at Old Trafford in September 1930 and a **7-3** rout at St James' Park in January 1960.
8. Newcastle have played in two great Premiership **seven-goal thrillers**. Kevin Keegan's Newcastle lost 4-3 to Liverpool in 1996, a game voted the Premiership's best ever. In October 2004, beat Kevin Keegan's Manchester City 4-3 at St James' Park.
9. On 1 September 1951, Newcastle beat Spurs **7-2**, with George Robledo scoring a hat-trick. Two weeks later, at United's next home game, they beat Burnley **7-1**.

10. George Robledo scored **seven** goals in a game against Border Province in South Africa in July 1952, still a club record.

11. The 1955 FA Cup final, which produced Newcastle's last domestic silverware, was played on **7 May**.

SHEARER QUOTE, UNQUOTE

The things said by – and about – the Geordie Boy

1. "He's the oldest 23-year-old I've ever met"

England dude David Platt is shocked by how mature his room-mate Alan Shearer is.

2. "The commission accepted that the incident was initially caused by Neil Lennon pulling at the shirt of Alan Shearer… It further accepted that the alleged incident of Alan Shearer swinging out with his left leg was a genuine attempt to free himself"

The FA wasn't at all swayed by Al's clean cut consummate pro image or the fact that he was an England regular when coming to this verdict in 2000.

3. "A person you'd be delighted to have as your son"

Says Kenny Dalglish.

4. "Alan Shearer is boring. We call him Mary Poppins"

Freddie Shepherd, in conversation with a fake sheikh who was really a *News of the World* reporter.

5. "He used to ring me to come and change the oil in his car. He can't even change a wheel"

Neil Ruddock reveals that Shearer would never have made it as a mechanic.

6. "At school I put down 'dustbin man' on my career questionnaire. My dad made me change it to joiner"

Shearer contemplating what he might have done if he hadn't played football.

7. "The money is a great bonus, don't get me wrong. But I would play for nothing. If I wasn't a pro, I would play on Sundays. It's a cliché but I just want to play football" The No9 opens up – a teeny bit – to *Loaded* magazine.

8. "Graeme has said he wants Alan to take over when he leaves and, as far as I

know, it's what our fans want. I've not said it before, but I am saying it now"
Freddy Shepherd makes amends for that Mary Poppins jibe.

9. "'Shearer stops me taking the throw-in. I lose it, throw the ball at him. 'You prick,' he sneers. The way he says it I know he means it. I go for him, try to grab him by the throat. He's grinning. He gestures dismissively. The red card comes out. Shearer's right. I am a prick. Fell into the trap"
Roy Keane reveals his respect for Shearer's gamesmanship in his autobiography.

10. "Happy birthday boss, any chance of a pay rise?"
Shearer's cheery card for manager Sir Bobby Robson on his 70th birthday.

11. "He's obsessive to the point it helps him, not so obsessive it's unhealthy"
Team-mate Graeme LeSaux on Shearer's attitude to football.

SHEER-AA!!!

Magic-Al moments

1. **July 1996** The Geordie boy finally gets his greatest wish and joins his home town club from Blackburn Rovers for £15m, then a world-record fee. Shearer had had a trial with Newcastle as a schoolboy but it didn't work out.

2. **August 1996** Scores his first goal for his beloved Newcastle United direct from a free-kick against Wimbledon. He was delighted it was in front of his own fans at St James' Park – even though it was the opposite end to where he stood as a kid.

3. **May 1997** Leads Newcastle to an FA Cup final at Wembley scoring five goals on the way. But there was to be no goal in the final, just a loser's medal.

4. **May 1998** Newcastle fans, on a daring dawn raid, drape a 29ft x 17ft Alan Shearer replica shirt over the Angel of the North. Sadly, even though the striker has bagged five more goals leading United to Wembley for a second successive FA Cup final, he still comes back with a loser's medal.

5. **September 1999** Shearer hits five as Sheffield Wednesday are beaten 8-0, while 36,000 fans sing "Walking in a Robson wonderland". The striker later admits that this was the game that saved his career, renewing his appetite for football.

6. **May 2000** Scores the 300th goal of an illustrious career – on the last day of the

season against Arsenal at St James' Park. Not a bad sign off before the summer.

7. March 2001 Had the Freedom of the City of Newcastle bestowed on him and three months later was awarded the OBE in the Queen's Birthday honours list. Not bad for a sheet-metal worker's son from Gosforth.

8. April 2002 Picked up the Barclaycard Merit Award for becoming the first player to reach the 200 mark in the Premiership following his goal against Charlton Athletic. No other player has yet reached this figure.

9. January 2003 His goal against Manchester City in just 10.25 seconds equalled the record as the fastest Premiership goal of all time.

10. February 2003 His first hat-trick since he put five past Wednesday demolishes Bayer Leverkusen and at least gives United a hope of reaching the last eight of the Champions League.

11. March 2003 Two goals against Inter Milan takes him level with 1920's goal-scoring legend Hughie Gallacher in terms of Newcastle career goals. A goal at Charlton sees him overtake him to secure third place in the all-time United goal scoring records. In April 2005, just nine goals short of Milburn's record, he announces he will play on for another season. Newcastle celebrate by losing their next game 3-0 to Aston Villa at St James' Park, with Bowyer and Dyer sent off.

SHIPPING GOALS

Seasons when United were most unsteady at the back

1. 1960/61 109 goals
2. 1929/30 92 goals
3. 1930/31 87 goals
   1931/32 87 goals
5. 1894/95 84 goals
   1991/92 84 goals
7. 1927/28 81 goals
   1957/58 81 goals
   1966/67 81 goals
10. 1958/59 80 goals
11. 1935/36 79 goals

SIT-INS AND OTHER UNUSUAL ENTERTAINMENTS

Supporting Newcastle can be diverting – even if the games aren't always

1. Paper planes
If you're going to watch Newcastle draw 0-0 with Crystal Palace at the end of a very miserable season (2004/05), you might as well have some fun. Newcastle fans pay tribute to Palace boss Iain Dowie's expertise in aeronautical engineering by using their origami skills to make some paper planes. One superbly targetted work of origami art lands near the penalty spot, earning the biggest cheer of the day.

2. Sliding draw
Although Newcastle won the last home game of 1997/98 3-1, beating Gianluca Vialli's Chelsea, the real highlight of the afternoon was the Chelsea fan who decided sliding down the bannister in the away end was more fun than watching the match. He had a point and, being reasonably skilled, was warmly applauded by all sides.

3. Hooligans for the Cup!
The Toon Army's pitch invasion, with Newcastle 3-1 down at St James' Park and just 30 minutes to go in the FA Cup sixth round, changes the course of the tie. The match is stopped for 12 minutes and, after the restart, Newcastle storm back to win 4-3. After some blazered shilly-shallying, the game is replayed, which satisfies nobody. Neutrals think Newcastle should be thrown out and we lose the 1974 final anyway.

4. "Now look here Mr Goalscorer…"
In the dark chasm that was the early 1990s, many fans handled adversity in different ways. Against Plymouth, in September 1991, with the Toon searching for their first home win, the mighty Argyle went 2-0 up and, after the second went in, a Newcastle fan had to be cleared from the pitch after giving the goalscorer a stern talking to.

5. The Good Friday riot
Try to squeeze 50-70,000 fans into a ground with a capacity of 30,000 – as St James' Park had in 1901 – with only 25 policemen on duty for a Tyne and Wear derby and you have the perfect recipe for a riot. The game had to be abandoned because there wasn't enough space on the pitch t play. Reinforced police took several hours – and baton charges – to clear the ground. But by then it had been partly demolished. Incredibly, only nine people required hospital treatment – and one of them was hit on the head by the crossbar he was trying to demolish.

6. There are some horses on the pitch… they think it's all over
Another fractious Tyne and Wear derby, at Roker Park in September 1909, is

nterrupted by Mackems after 13 minutes as Albert Shepherd gives United the lead. Mounted police restore order and the game resumes after 12 minutes. At one point, the players have to scatter as one horse gallops across the pitch. Newcastle score again to win 2-0 and go top of the league.

7. Galvin goes wild

At the end of September 1991, Newcastle entertain Arthur Cox's Derby County. The frantic 2-2 draw is not as intriguing – or as hotly contested – as the battle between the dugouts, a battle culminating when Newcastle assistant coach Tony Galvin kicks a bucket of water over Cox and his assistants and has to be forcibly restrained, after trying to attack them with a wooden bench.

8. A family affair

United fans are so surprised to see Frank Clark fire the ball into the net against Doncaster Rovers in the 1973/74 League Cup that they run onto the pitch in ecstatic celebration. The first fan to congratulate Clark is his brother-in-law.

9. The young Geordie dancer

A 1-1 draw in the November 1991 Tyne and Wear derby is enlivened, briefly, when a small boy, wearing a black and white scarf, dances across the Roker Park pitch.

10. Spot the protestor

One fan is so appalled by United's performance in a 1-0 defeat at home to Wrexham in November 1980, that he sits on the centre-spot in protest, and is escorted off the pitch to a round of boos.

11. A different kind of sit-in

Len Shackleton decides United's 4-1 win over Cardiff in November 1947 would not be complete without some flagrant exhibitionism. So, after playing one-twos with the corner flag, he decided to sit on the ball – a feat which obviously inspired, a generation or so later, the great Kenny Wharton.

SPARTAN HEROES

11 who came – or went to – Blyth Spartans

1. **Derek Bell** Newcastle United 1981-83; Blyth Spartans 1994, 1995
2. **Ray 'Bomber' Blackhall** Newcastle United 1973-78; Blyth Spartans 1984
3. **John Brownlie** Newcastle United 1978-82; Blyth Spartans 1986

4. John Burridge Newcastle United 1989-91; later goalkeeping coach, Blyth Spartans August 1996
5. Steve Carney Newcastle United 1979-85; Blyth Spartans 1987-90
6. Kevin Carr Newcastle United 1976-85; Blyth Spartans 1988-89
7. Peter Cartwright Newcastle United 1979-83; Blyth Spartans 1984-87
8. David Craig Newcastle United 1960-78; Blyth Spartans 1978
9. Ron Guthrie Newcastle United 1963-73, Blyth Spartans 1977
10. Joe Richardson Blyth Spartans – no one seems to know for how long – but joined Newcastle in 1929 and, as player and trainer, stayed at the club until 1977.
11. Alan Shoulder Blyth Spartans 1977; Newcastle United 1978-82

The biggest gate of the 1977/78 season at St James' Park was not for a United game but for Blyth Spartans FA Cup fifth round replay against Wrexham. The crowd was officially estimated at 42,000, but many more were locked out.

SPORTING SUPERSTARS

Weightlifters, bowls internationals, boxers – and all Newcastle players

1. Harry Hardinge
A Newcastle reserve in the 1900s, Harry Hardinge is the only Newcastle United centre-forward to score over 1,000 runs in a cricket season 18 times. He won one England cap as a footballer in 1910 and another as a batsman in 1921. In 1915 he was voted Wisden Cricketer of the Year.

2. Jesse Carver
Writers invariably described this Newcastle centre-half as sturdy, but then Jesse had been a champion weightlifter.

3. Robert Aitken
Represented Great Britain schools at basketball.

4. John Bailey
An intelligent defender, who starred for Newcastle in the 1980s, competed in the ABA boxing championships.

5. Ronald Williams
Starring at centre-forward in the 1930s, was capped by Wales in 1976 as a bowls player.

11. ST JAMES' PARK PIONEERS

David Whitton

Harry Jeffery   James Miller

Bobby   Willie Graham   Joe McKane   James
Creilly   Collins

Tom   Willie Thompson Joseph Wallace Jock
Crate   Sorley

The 11 who played for
Newcastle East End against
Celtic in the first game at
St James' Park on 3
September 1892

6. Paul Gascoigne
The boy genius represented his school at tennis, playing in a white T-shirt and black Newcastle shorts because his parents couldn't afford the tennis strip.

7. David Hollins
Brother of John, the Chelsea star, Dave played bowls for the London Welsh club after keeping goal got too much for him.

8. Malcolm Scott
A solid defender who could play upfront but he may have been an even better cricketer. On the books of Northamptonshire and Durham, he was a useful spin bowler even if, in 1967, he was banned for an illegal action.

9. Thomas Ghee
A stern, uncompromising skipper for Newcastle at the turn of the century, who was an extremely adept swimmer and water polo player.

10. Bill Appleyard
Striker Appleyard loved to play billiards, becoming the footballers' champion billiard

player and starring in exhibition matches in the north-east in the 1900s.

11. Arthur Turner
A fast, flair player for Newcastle in 1903/04, he played cricket for clubs in Hampshire.

STRIKE RATES

The 11 strikers with the best strike rate (who have scored 50 goals or more)

1. Hughie Gallacher 143 goals in 174 games, 82 per cent
2. Andy Cole 68 goals in 84 games, 81 per cent
3. Albert Shepherd 92 goals in 123 games, 75 per cent
4. Jack Smith 73 goals in 112 games, 65 per cent
5. Barrie Thomas 50 goals in 78 games, 64 per cent
6. Les Ferdinand 50 goals in 83 games, 62 per cent
   Bill Appleyard 87 goals in 145 games, 60 per cent
8. Billy Cairns 53 goals in 90 games, 59 per cent
9. Jock Peddie 78 goals in 136 games, 58 per cent
10. Len White 153 goals in 269 games, 57 per cent
11. Vic Keeble 67 goals in 120 games, 56 per cent

STRIPPING YARNS

11 did you knows? about Newcastle's strip

1. Newcastle East End, one of the clubs that united to form the Magpies, played in red shirts and, er, red and white stripes. These kits were discarded on April 1894 because of frequent colour clashes with other Division Two sides.

2. Newcastle West End, the other club merged into United, played in various kits, notably red and black/dark blue hooped shirts.

3. In April 1894, the board's journal noted: "It was agreed that the club's colours be changed from red shirts and white knickers to black and white shirts (two inch stripe) and dark knickers."

4. The most popular explanation for this mysterious choice is that the club was fervently supported by a Dutch monk, Father Dalmatius Houtman, whose monastery was just a goal-kick away from the club. On his many visits to the ground to meet players, he wore a traditional black and white monk's habit.

5. Those unconvinced the club was inspired by Father Houtman's habit go back to the English Civil War. The Cavalier William Cavendish (1592-1676), who was Earl – and later Duke – of Newcastle had black and white colours. The Royalist army he raised on Tyneside had white shirts, dark trousers and hats, with black boots – a colour scheme which might make them the very first Toon Army.

6. Others insist the colours were inspired by a pair of magpies who nested in the Victorian Stand at St James' Park.

7. United wore dark blue shorts in many games before World War 1.

8. In 1958/59, Charlie Mitten tried to make the kit look more continental but it was regarded, club historian Paul Joannou noted, as "almost effeminate".

9. The next radical innovation was the famous bar code kit – a mix of narrow and broad black and white stripes – launched in 1989/90. Briefly popular with fans in the 1980s was the Brazil kit worn in honour of Mirandinha.

10. Against Monaco, in the 1996/97 Champions League, Newcastle weren't allowed to wear their standard kit, which had a beautiful big Newcastle Brown Ale logo in the middle, as such shirt sponsorship was banned in France. So they wore a kit with a Center Parks logo. NTL's logo has since replaced the Brown Ale mark on Newcastle's shirts but most fans nostalgically prefer the Brown Ale kit.

11. Ruud Gullit experimented with lucky white socks but they were so lucky he left in August 1999 after a year in charge. Another lucky kit – the lucky yellow away kit – failed to live up to its billing in the 2004/05 UEFA Cup quarter-final in Lisbon. With 20 minutes to go, United are 1-0 up on the night, 2-0 up on aggregate, but lose the game 4-1 – United's last hope of silverware is gone for the 36th season in a row. You've got to admit, that's one heck of a lucky away strip.

11 SUPERMAC MOMENTS

The daring deeds of Tyneside's very own superhero

1. "Supermac, superstar, how many goals have you scored so far?"
The best thing Tim Rice and Andrew Lloyd Webber have done for Newcastle…

2. The fastest ever goal?
In a friendly away to St Johnstone in July 1972, Supermac scored what might have been the fastest goal ever in the club's – or the game's – history. Kicking off, John Tudor tapped it to Supermac who belted it from 55 yards into the net. The goal was unofficially timed at five seconds.

3. Supermac destroys Burnley
His first goal in the 1974 FA Cup semi-final against Burnley was pretty good – he ignored Colin Waldron's wrestling to score from the rebound after Stevenson had saved his first shot – but the second was even better, possibly because it involved four of the greatest stars of that side. Moncur headed a loose ball out to the edge of the box, Tudor flicked it on to Hibbit whose long first-time pass found Supermac perfectly. Burnley manager Jimmy Adamson said afterwards: "He must have goals imprinted on his heart."

4. "Technically I was wrong"
Against Leicester in April 1975, Irving Nattrass races down the left with the ball, while four of his team-mates sprint through midfield to keep up. The squared pass baffles Leicester's defence but falls invitingly for Supermac. "I just hit it from 30 yards. Technically I was wrong but it felt good from the moment it left my foot and was still going up when it went into the top corner."

5. Two hours late, in a chauffeur-driven Rolls
That was how Supermac arrived at St James' Park for his medical in May 1971. Critics wondered if this converted full-back from Luton Town could live up to all the hype. So what did Supermac do? Generate even more hype and then lived up to it, scoring a stunning volley on a pre-season friendly against St Etienne and grabbing a hat-trick on his home debut.

6. A nap against Cyprus
Supermac remains the only player to score five in one match for England – albeit against Cyprus in April 1975. Kevin Keegan, playing upfront alongside Macdonald, recalls: "He knocked me out of the way for one of them. I was set to score when he barged me aside and headed in. He was in the mood to score 20 and yet strangely,

the match that made him finished him. He never recovered that scoring touch for England." The goal times, for the record, were: 2, 35, 48, 53, 86.

7. Supermac the local hero
He may have been born in Luton, but Macdonald became the biggest Geordie icon since Jackie Milburn. One of his many fans was Mark Knopfler, whose theme to the movie *Local Hero* is now the matchday anthem at St James' Park. While *Local Hero* seems an appropriate anthem for Supermac, there have been times in United's history when the name of Knopfler's band would have seemed even more appropriate: Dire Straits.

8. "A popular lad until he climbs into bed…"
Keegan's verdict on Supermac in their England years together. He was, Keegan recalls, "a window-rattling snorer. Wherever England stayed, Malcolm was always banished to the farthest room in the hotel."

9. "I'm the fourth best finisher I've ever seen…"
The first three, in case you were wondering, being Jimmy Greaves, Denis Law and Bryan 'Pop' Robson.

10. A fan writes…
"The best begging letter I ever received came after Newcastle had won through to the 1974 FA Cup final. It just said simply: 'I was conceived while my mother waited in a Cup Final queue, surely I am entitled to a ticket?'"

11. TV times
Supermac admits that he can't bear to watch television over the first weekend of any January. "I know they'll trot out the Hereford match as a stick to beat Newcastle over the head with." He remembers Ronnie Radford's strike for Hereford better than most: "The ball sat up on a divot for him. He'd never struck a ball like that before and he never did again." But, as the great sideburned philosopher says: "Football is a stupid game. Having lost to Hereford we went to Old Trafford and gave Manchester United a thrashing."

TEAMS WE LOVE TO HATE

Astonishingly, they're not all called Sunderland

1. Sunderland
For obvious reasons. If they're not obvious see Mackem Moments.

2. Leeds United
The rivalry intensified when Don Revie's Leeds were in their pomp and, in 1968, Jack Charlton and John McNamee engaged in a personal war as the Peacocks won 1-0. With Sunderland and Boro both out of the top flight, Leeds became the nearest local derby for a while in the 1970s and there was much fan violence. Shearer is our top scorer against Leeds with 12 goals, while Norman Hunter and Michael Duberry have both scored own goals for Newcastle in this fixture, so thanks guys.

3. Arsenal
Because they are too successful by half, there's often crowd trouble at the Library and have the cruellest jokes about the Toon Army being unemployed.

4. Manchester United
They nicked the title from us, with a little help from our defence.

5. Chelsea
Wrecking Roman Abramovich's dreams of a Treble was very satisfying. There has been a fair trade in players between the clubs over the years – we gave them Hughie Gallacher and Roy Bentley, they gave us Babayaro. Chelsea have shot up the list because they've got Abramovich and we haven't and because they marked the 50th anniversary of their one league title by winning the Premiership; United celebrated the 50th anniversary of our FA Cup win by getting stuffed in the semis.

6. Barcelona

Because they were extremely arrogant – Louis van Gaal said United were over-age and overrated – when they came to St James' Park in September 1997, fully deserving to be humbled. They've not always been so mighty. Let's not forget: they drew twice with Crook Town in 1913.

7. Hartlepool United

Because they're virtually Mackems by any other name.

8. The Boro

The Smoggies would like us to hate them more than we do but we don't really.

9. Stevenage Borough

Arsey buggers – ideas above their station.

10. Birmingham City

An absurd number of games between United and Brum's finest – six in six weeks in 1973/74 in all competitions – led to serious niggling, especially after Jim Smith broke a City player's leg in two places. In the sixth game, Paul Hendrie and, to a lesser extent, Kenny Burns simply ran amok for City, leaving holes in opponents' shins, ending Irving Nattrass's season with a bad foul. Birmingham won, but even their manager Freddie Goodwin called for an ice-hockey sin bin to get tough on players.

11. Partizan Belgrade

Awkward buggers in Europe.

THANKS FOR THE MEMORIES KEV

In honour of the "thanks for the memories" banner let's just replay the greatest moments in King Kev's reign as a player and a manager

1. Royal Antwerp

"As good a one-off performance as I've seen in European football," according to Terry McDermott who has won three European Cups with Liverpool. Two up after eight minutes, three up by half-time, a headed hat-trick by Robert Lee. Genius.

2. Signing Alan Shearer

One summer, while he was at Blackburn, Shearer came back home to Gosforth and decided he wanted to look at the new St James' Park. He drove around and around

The line up for Keegan's Newcastle debut against QPR on 28 August 1982

The line up in his first game as manager against Bristol City on 8 February 1992

the ground – it was at that point that it became clear that one day he would play for United. But Keegan made it happen.

3. Howay 5-0h!
Just a pity less than 37,000 fans watched this 5-0 victory over Manchester United in person. When you thought about it, it didn't make up for gifting them the title in 1995/96 but, for a while, it felt like payback. As John Beresford says, "Everything clicked that day." The video of the game puns on the *Hawaii Five-0* TV show.

4. 4-0
The highlight of this humbling of Ferencvaros in the 1996/97 UEFA Cup was a sublime goal from Ginola. Lurking on the edge of the area in the 90th minute, the Frenchman brought the ball down and hit an astonishing volley into the roof of the net. It was the kind of goal you only normally score in training.

5. Joining Newcastle in August 1982

Within 24 hours of his arrival, the queues for season tickets stretched around the streets of Gallowgate. Then 33, Keegan said his only regret was that he hadn't played for Newcastle sooner. Manager Arthur Cox put it best: "No other player in the world could have had such a dramatic effect on the club and its supporters."

6. The training sessions

Open to the public, more entertaining than most lower league games and attracting similar crowds. And the autographs – always signed without a quibble.

7. A grand exit

Nobody who saw Keegan leave the north-east from the centre of St James' Park in a helicopter in May 1984 will ever forget it. Some footballers hang up their boots quietly, others leave in a manner normally reserved for movie stars, pop legends and national saviours. It was over the top, heartbreaking, yet oddly exhilarating.

8. Seventh heaven

The last game of 1992/93, Newcastle have already won the old First Division so the result, against Leicester City, doesn't really matter. Most teams might take it easy but Keegan's men are 6-0 up at half-time – the first time the club has scored six in one half since 1946 – and win 7-1 with Andy Cole and David Kelly grabbing hat-tricks, the first time two United players have scored three in the same game since 1946.

9. "Craggs forward, Varadi, Keegan again, chance here for Keegan… he's done it! Kevin Keegan scores and St James' Park goes absolutely wild"

Roger Tames describing Keegan's debut goal for Newcastle against QPR in 1982. It was two minutes before the ref could restart the game. Among those who queued for five hours to get into the Gallowgate was a 12-year-old called Alan Shearer.

10. 3-4

As sometimes happened with King Kev, United lost this seven-goal thriller in April 1996 against Liverpool, a match invariably described the best Premiership game ever. Still, better to lose a game like this than in the familiar listless witless manner of some more recent defeats.

11. The resurrection starts here

Keegan's first game as manager of Newcastle United, against Bristol City, on 8 February 1992 sees the crowd almost double – to 29,263. The omens aren't especially brilliant – Newcastle are defending like a sieve and Lee Clark has swung at a team-mate in training and been dropped by Keegan. United win 3-0, ending a six-game streak without a win and marking the first clean sheet in a dozen league games. After one game, the Third Division doesn't seem so inevitable after all.

THERE ARE ONLY 11 NEWCASTLES

Footballing Newcastles starting with the greatest

1. Newcastle United
2. Newcastle FC They beat Manchester United to win the Gibraltar league in 2004/05 for the second year in a row.
3. Newcastle Rangers This club died so that United could be born.
4. Newcastle West End When West End met East End, United were formed…
5. Newcastle East End
6. Newcastle Town Quite big in the North West Counties League.
7. Newcastle United Jets New South Wales team, hitherto known as the Newcastle Breakers, whose hardcore fans were dubbed the Rowdies.
8. Newcastle Emlyn Doyens of the Welsh third division.
9. Newcastle Blue Star Northern League second division side who briefly changed their name to Newcastle RTM. Steve Carney managed them from 1992 to 1996.
10. Newcastle City Expunged, the records say, from the Wearside league in 1994/95.
11. Newcastle Benfield Saints Formerly Newcastle Benfield Park, they have found a niche in the Northern League.

THEY ALSO PLAY IN BLACK AND WHITE STRIPES

The zebra look is popular the world over

1. Juventus Let's face it, they've been almost as successful as us.
2. Notts County Apparently it's their fault that Juve don't have a pink home strip.
3. Shepshed Dynamo Crazy name, not such a crazy team. Gave a lippy upstart called Martin O'Neill his start in management.
4. Brockham Badgers In remote rural Surrey, a few small villages in and around the Mole Valley have teams called Badgers who play in the colours of the beast and are always being persecuted by local farmers.
5. Grimsby Town Like they say in Yorkshire, Grimsby isn't the end of the world – but you can see it from there.
6. Montevideo Wanderers They're over 100 years old, they're in Uruguay and they haven't won very much.

7. Partizan Belgrade Beat us and gave Real Madrid a good fright in the Champions League in 2003/04.

8. LASK Linz "Die Schwarz Weissen" – the black and whites – languish near the bottom of Austria's Division one after being relegated from the Austrian Bundesliga.

9. Wick Academy The Scorries are the northernmost team in the Highland League.

10. RS Charleroi A chap called Philippe Albert played for this Belgian side once.

11. Lokomotiv Plovdiv Bulgarian challengers for honours who probably endure an awful lot of transport-related puns from Bulgarian football commentators.

TIME GENTLEMEN PLEASE!

After calling time on their playing days, this team of Newcastle United players headed straight to the bar, as a pub landlord not a customer

John Barker
John Carr
Alexander Gardner
George Wilson Heslop
Terry Hibbitt
Malcolm Macdonald
Albert Shepherd
John Smith
James Stott
James Thomson
Tommy Wright

TINO, TINO, OH TINO

You can sing it to the tune of Dexy's Midnight Runners' Geno if you want. Or not

1. "Three goals – not bad"
The mercurial Colombian genius's rather laid-back appraisal of his hat-trick against Barcelona in the 1997 Champions League.

2. Tino's dad
It was always a treat to see Tino Senior turn up at St James' Park to watch his boy. He had an endearing habit of laughing hysterically whenever a player from either side made a mistake. And, like his son, he seemed to live in a world of his own.

3. A double against Metz

Two goals in two minutes in the dying stages against Metz in the 1996/97 UEFA Cup clinched the tie. It was somehow typically Tino that the Colombian was then booked for taking his shirt off in celebration and pulled a hamstring.

4. "Vaya cuidad – what a town!"

Tino's amazed reaction after paying his first visit to Bigg Market. He was said to be very impressed by the fact that women wore mini-skirts in Newcastle in winter. He wanted to get a fishing boat so they took him to Tynemouth the first weekend he was here. He took one look at the North Sea and said "F**k that".

5. The humiliation of Everton

Not quite up there with his heroics against Barça, but Tino turned this game around in magnificent fashion. With Everton 1-0 up at half-time, Asprilla came on in the 57th minute, teed up Rob Lee for Newcastle's second goal and so bewitched Claus Thomsen the Everton defender felt the only way he could stop a mazy dribble was to upend him in the penalty area. Shearer scored from the spot. The 4-1 rout was completed with a scrambled injury-time goal by Robbie Elliott. But it was Tino's triumph – even if he didn't get on the scoresheet.

6. "Cockroaches taste like roasted peanuts"

Take it from Tino, who has been there, eaten them, on Colombian TV's equivalent to *I'm A Celebrity Get Me Out Of Here*. Alas, he was voted off after being plotted against by a local soap star. The only reason Tino went on the show, he said, "was to get my name out there and come back to football." He is still only 35, so don't rule him out.

7. Fleeing Darlington

Ambitious, publicity-hungry chairman George Reynolds thought he'd pulled off his biggest coup when he secured a work permit for Asprilla to play for Darlo. But just before he was due to be unveiled, the Colombian headed to the Middle East doing, in Reynold's words, "a runner at 5am". Tino did later apologise. Apparently he and George couldn't agree personal terms.

8. "How are you?"

The three words of English that Tino definitely could speak when he joined Newcastle in February 1996. He soon augmented these with a few chat-up lines.

9. Down by the Riverside

Brought on for his debut against Middlesbrough in February 1996, Tino ran down the left-wing, baffled Boro's defence and crossed for Steve Watson to equalise.